HAVING MY WAY

LEONARD E. READ

HAVING MY WAY

The Foundation for Economic Education, Inc.
Irvington-on-Hudson, New York 10533
1974

ABOUT THE PUBLISHER

The Foundation for Economic Education is a non-political, nonprofit, educational institution. Its senior staff and numerous writers are students as well as teachers of the free market, private ownership, limited government rationale. Sample copies of the Foundation's monthly study journal, *The Freeman,* are available on request.

Published March 1974

(paper) ISBN-0-910614-50-4
(cloth) ISBN-0-910614-49-0

To
Benjamin A. Rogge
and those others who make their lights
as bright as they can be

CONTENTS

1. HOW I MAY HAVE MY OWN WAY   1

If my ways be right, I cannot fail; if wrong, I cannot succeed.

2. HUMILITY: THE WAY OF FREEDOM   7

Freedom is possible when a sense of awe and a spirit of inquiry displace authoritarian attitudes and practices.

3. THE MEEK SHALL INHERIT THE EARTH   12

The teachable shall be graced with a realization of their earthly potentialities.

4. LIFE STYLES   17

Trends are upgraded as one discovers himself and sets a better style.

5. SHOEMAKER, STICK TO YOUR LAST 24

Look not to self-proclaimed "specialists" for the structuring of a good society, for that is everyman's task.

6. THE BLESSINGS OF ADVERSITY 30

Adversity activates talents which in prosperous times lie dormant.

7. APPEAL TO THE INTELLECT 36

People tend to rise to the intelligence expected of them, but if adjudged to be ignorant, will slump accordingly.

8. AWAIT DISCOVERY 40

Patience! Enlightenment will draw the seekers of light.

9. SAY WHAT YOU MEAN 45

You can reflect another's viewpoint, but can radiate only that which is your own.

10. THE CONFESSION OF ERROR 49

Truth lies beyond a double door: the discernment of error and open confession to self and others.

11. PENALTY OF SURRENDER 54

In matters of principle, avoid compromise; for a principle is surrendered if not strictly observed.

12. WORSHIP, A SINGULAR THING 63

Beware of idolizing others and of those who would worship you.

13. THE FEAR OF FREEDOM 68

One can be free only when self-responsible, but the thought of it is frightening.

14. INEQUALITY ENSHRINED 76

Equality before the law is simple justice, but the richness of our lives derives from our differences.

15. THE REVEALING SELF 84

Not the ideas one propounds but the examples he sets reveal his true nature.

16. RAILING AGAINST FOLLY 88

Struggling against the errors of others is time taken from one's own upgrading.

17. TIME-LAPSE THINKING   93

The best way to judge whether a present action is
right or wrong is to assess its long-range effect.

18. BUY AMERICAN   97

Let those who insist on a "Made in America"
label concentrate on the American concept of
voluntary exchange.

19. REVERENCE, THAT ANGEL OF THE WORLD   104

Reverence for human life involves respect for
animals and plants as well.

20. SISYPHUS   112

A bit of economic enlightenment from Greek
mythology through that amazing Frenchman,
Frederic Bastiat.

21. EVIL BEGUN, RARELY UNDONE   115

The way to cure bad habits and wrong methods
is to avoid them in the beginning.

22. THE GLORY OF WORK   122

Instead of an unfortunate necessity, work is a
glorious means of realizing life's highest goals.

23. EMPLOYMENT REDEFINED   129

If employment is nothing more than job occupancy, then perhaps the socialist way is best!

24. HOW TO STOP INFLATION   134

Excessive government spending can never be curbed in the face of excessive demands on government.

25. HOW NOT TO BE OWNED   142

To avoid slavery, one must learn the freedom philosophy and how to live by it.

26. IF I WERE KING   148

Never assume powers of control you would not freely grant to anyone else; this is one key to limited government.

27. THE RIGHT TO QUIT   152

The right to quit and the right to start are basic aspects of the right to life.

28. THE ROLE OF INTERFERENCE   157

Clearly define which actions of individuals shall be considered injurious to others and you will then know the proper limits of government.

29. HARMONY UNDERSTOOD   163

Without a lodestar—the ideal of a harmonious and free society—we are adrift and without compass.

INDEX   171

THE REMNANT

In every society there are people who have the intelligence to figure out the requirements of liberty and the character to walk in its ways. There is a Remnant! This is a scattered fellowship of individuals bound together by a love of ideas and a hunger to know the plain truth of things. The idea of working with such people is intriguing, but how does one establish contact? The Remnant resists the hard sell, or any other kind of sell; they refuse to be fetched. Any suspicion that they might be the target of someone's efforts and they vanish. Nevertheless, it is possible to work with The Remnant, and no task is more rewarding. There's only one way to go about it: Let a man cultivate his own garden, and if he produces anything worthwhile, he may be sure, as Albert Jay Nock says, "that The Remnant will find him. He may rely on that with absolute assurance. They will find him without his doing anything about it; in fact, if he tries to do anything about it, he is pretty sure to put them off...."

1

HOW I MAY HAVE MY OWN WAY

Let him that would save the world
first move himself.

—SOCRATES

It seems that nearly everyone has an instinctive desire to have his own way. Too often this becomes insistent and shows forth as "Do as I say, or else!" No two desires are alike, and this tendency of each to insist on having his own way may well be a major source of conflict and disharmony in society. Now, if I read man's purpose aright, we should be heading toward harmonious rather than conflicting relationships, and something unintelligent goes on here if one of man's instinctive desires is hostile to his life's purpose. It is for this reason that I wish to think through for myself how I can have my own way and, at the same time, do no injury or injustice to others—indeed, be an asset to them. If I can find a way to live like this, then others can also.

Perhaps the answer will come clear if I can resolve two other questions: Who am I? and Where am I going? Or, better yet, What really is my way? Another phrasing of these questions might be: What is man's nature? and What is man's destiny? These speculations are as ancient as man himself. Although they may be beyond the capacity of any person to answer, some light may be shed as one wrestles with them.

Who am I? This question is seldom raised because most answers to it are so vague. Such a question falls into the same unfathomable category as Who or What is God or Creation? Nonetheless, it is interesting to speculate, for one comes upon this anomaly: I am next to nothing and yet a part of everything. Infinitesimal though I be, I am phased into the Infinite!

Who am I? Here's one part of the answer: I am one octillion atoms—1,000,000,000,000,000,000,000,000,000—a number difficult to grasp unless we use the imagination. Cover the surface of this earth—and the seas—with dried peas to a depth of four feet and that would fall far, far short of an octillion. Go out into the universe and cover 250,000 other earth-sized planets with four feet of peas and that would be the number of atoms in my make up.[1]

The atom? It is so small that 30 trillion atoms could be placed on the period at the end of this sentence without overlapping. Blow it up to 100 yards in diameter and what do you behold? Radiant energy in the form of electrons, neutrons, and the like, in wave sequences flying about at the speed of light. In the center is the atomic nucleus which, after being thus expanded, is the size of a pinhead. This and this alone is "stuff," and no one knows what it is, except that it appears "solid." All else is empty space.

---

[1]See "The New Science and The New Faith" by Dr. Donald Hatch Andrews, *The Freeman*, April 1961.

Were it possible to apply an atomic press to me and squeeze out all but the "stuff,"—the nuclei—I would be a particle so small that it would not be discernible on a piece of white paper. In a word, I am but a mere speck—next to nothing!

As for the other side of the coin, there is a sense in which I am more than a mere, mechanistic speck—infinitely more. For instance, my octillion atoms are not the same atoms they were a few years ago. They continuously escape and a new octillion enters about every five years. To where do they escape and from whence come the new ones? To and from everywhere throughout the universe! As the famous chemist, Dr. Andrews, writes:

There is a high probability that you have in your body right now a thousand atoms that were once in the body of Julius Caesar. . . . And speaking very reverently, we can say that each of us has in his body a thousand atoms that were in the body of Christ . . . the individual atoms are scarcely more than the shadows of a far deeper reality that we find in this total atomic *harmony* within us, the spirit of our Creator within us.

If I wave my hand . . . it not only moves the leaves on the trees outside, creates ripples down on the water of the bay, but also moves the moon; the sun feels this motion, and the stars; even the farthest nebula will tremble because of the motion of my hand. As a famous physicist put it, every heartbeat is felt through the entire universe.

. . . there is in each of us an eternal core, call it dynamic force, call it personality, call it spirit or soul or symphony or what you will; there is in us this core, this director of our symphony of life that somehow has an invariance that transcends the changes of space and time. And in this way, we can understand that in mortal life there is this immortal reality that merges with the eternal.[2]

So, I am next to nothing—and a part of everything—as is every human being. That's who and what you are and I am!

Like almost everyone else, I want to have my own way. Is this possible? Yes, if my way be right; indeed, having one's own way is not only possible but certain if the way be right, and just as certainly impossible if the way be wrong. Thus, having one's own way or not revolves around right and wrong behavior. While few matters stand more in contention than right and wrong, I have a way of drawing the line that suits me.

Wrote Thoreau, "If I knew for a certainty that a man was coming to my house with the conscious design of doing me good, I should run for my life." When anyone attempts to run the life of another, to mold the other to his own design, to cast anyone else in his own image—regardless of intent, be it degrading or generous—the other should indeed run for his life. Why? It is this domineering trait that arouses conflict and disharmony in society and accounts for the taking of lives by the millions.

If making carbon copies of others be one's intention, he will never have his own way. It is impossible; it cannot be done. Point to a single success! The one dominated is resentful, and well he might be. Any respect he may have had gives way to disfavor, even hate. And the dominator is no less harmed; he not only views the failures at his own hand but, if he has any sense at all, he notes that in attempting to run the lives of others he has neglected to control and improve his own life.

---

[2]*Ibid.*

Thus does the harm spread in both directions, whether it stems from a private dictocrat lording it over only one other or, as we are seeing more and more, political dictocrats lording it over millions! Not a one of them will have his own way.

Very well! What is the right way as I see it? I take my cue from Socrates: "Let him that would save the world first move himself." In a word, I have not been given the world to save; you are not my target, nor is anyone else. Who then? Just me—that person who is at once next to nothing and a part of everything!

To help keep myself on target, I have embraced a few guidelines, for which I claim no originality:

- Interfere with no one's creative actions.
- Do not to others that which I would not have them do to me.
- Extend respect and kindness to others, even when they appear to be wrong.
- Share my recipes for living, cooking, or whatever with anyone who cares to know.
- Strive for the perfection of my own goods and/or services and exchange with others when mutually advantageous.
- Maintain enthusiasm and curiosity.
- Yield not to stress and hardship.
- Profit from error by open confession.
- Condone no special privilege for self or others.
- Let all proclaimed positions be an accurate reflection of whatever my highest conscience dictates as right—integrity.
- Seek truth, play fair with everyone, learn teamwork.

What then is required to have my own way? Nothing more than to practice the kind of self-control which aligns individual lives with the master pattern. Anyone who cannot so master his own life does not deserve to have his own way.

Finally, consider how a more or less general practice of such ways would lead away from conflict and toward harmony in society, that is, toward man's destiny. The way of personal improvement in peace and harmony—the way of freedom—is an open road uncluttered by man-made barriers.

*   *   *

The following chapters were written in answer to various questions—all relevant to the freedom theme—that have been raised in recent months. Old questions, old answers—so why not forget them? Strange as it may seem, they are important to me primarily because of questions that will be raised during coming months!

Time after time I have been stumped by a question that has popped into my head, and then thought it through for myself. Almost invariably, an inquiring soul, shortly thereafter, has raised the identical question. What goes on here? I do not know. In any event, how satisfying it is to reply with a carefully considered answer rather than a hasty and stumbling effort.

It is a pleasure to share these thoughts along the way with anyone who cares to listen.

2

HUMILITY:
THE WAY OF FREEDOM

The spirit of God delights to dwell
in the hearts of the humble.
—ERASMUS

No person known to me has more than scratched the surface in making the case for human freedom. It is not for the lack of valiant effort; thousands are trying, and their efforts range from name-calling to masterful expositions of the principles of political economy—yet with little if any success. We have been missing the boat; we simply have not hit upon the way. It is time to search beyond our normal explorations.

I am convinced that the route to human freedom is largely psychological, consisting in an awareness of and an adherence to that which is beyond the physical or material. True, this is an ancient idea, but it may sound strange to many in this day and age:

This influx in the mind [insight, intuition, discovery, invention, and so on] seems to me to be something I receive. I do not seem to generate it myself. If it came from me, I would suspect it; I would doubtless see it as a rationaliza-

7

tion of my own hidden desires and aspirations. . . . This is
something fresh and apart—not me. This is life flowing.
This is life in a rhythm of incessant flowing and ascension.
What is it? Who knows? "There is something," as Emerson said; and that is all I need by way of philosophy. *There
is something, and it works.*[1]

In this passage, Emerson and Dillaway were describing
something in the Cosmic Order over and beyond their own
minds or anyone else's. This "something" has been and is
variously referred to as God, Jehovah, Brahma, the Creator
or Creation, Infinite Intelligence or Mind or Consciousness.
No one can catalogue the Infinite; we may know *that* it is
but not *what* it is. It is beyond mundane categories, which is
the point of the second Commandment: "Thou shalt not make
unto thee any graven image. . . ." In a word, there is indeed a
mysterious Universal Power, but no more than an awareness of its presence is possible. Awareness, however, is all
that is necessary.

A concept or idea is not to be summarily dismissed simply
for being mysterious! Dig below the surface of the commonplace and mystery is there. No one knows what electricity is.
Yet, we are aware of this form of radiant energy and harness
it to our use. Our understanding of gravitation scratches the
surface, and the same goes for memory, the atom, the sun in
our galaxy, a lily, or the human cortex.

Let us recognize this fact: of none of these things—any
more than of God—do we have more than an inkling of its
nature! These everyday samplings of the Universal Power
come to seem commonplace in our experience, and so we fail

[1] See *Consent* by Newton Dillaway (Unity Village, Mo.: Unity Books,
1967), p. 27.

to recognize that our knowledge of them consists of mere inklings: we behave as if *we* were the Source, as if they were of our own hand. The Source—the Universal Power, whatever it is—is not thought to be of our own hand and, as a consequence, is often derided as sheer mysticism. Actually, this Source is no more esoteric than are any of its trillions of manifestations: all forms of life, a raindrop, the ring of your phone, a pencil, or power steering.

I am beginning to appreciate the importance of Voltaire's pronouncement to Frederick the Great:

> If God did not exist it would be necessary to invent Him. But all Nature cries aloud that He does exist, that there is a supreme intelligence, an immense power, an admirable order and everything teaches us our own dependence on it.

Dependence? Human freedom is out of the question in the absense of this awareness, that is, without a profound belief that there is "something" over and beyond our finite minds. Why? Humility, *in this unique sense,* is an absolute prerequisite to freedom, and it cannot function in the soul of man when he falls into the error of believing that ideas and material blessings are of his own little hand. The achievement of humility is the key to our problem's solution. I am suggesting that the way of humility is the way to freedom—the way we have been overlooking.[2]

What is humility in its highest sense? It is knowing that one's knowledge is imperfect or incomplete. Inklings, yes; all-

---

[2]Admittedly, were everyone humble in this unique sense, and utterly lacking in other virtues such as integrity, initiative, and so on, they could be free and still perish. It is my belief, however, that the other virtues tend to sprout and bloom when this kind of humility is mastered.

wise, never! Humility, as here used, is an awareness that the individual is not the originator but only the receiver of intelligence. Recognized is the fact that man, at best, only *intercepts* or tunes in understanding, truth, wisdom flowing from "something" higher than himself. This awareness is the essence of humility.

Man is not the Almighty and, in all humility, should know it. According to Erasmus, the spirit of God delights to dwell in those so graced. Goethe, using still another term for this "something," further clarifies the meaning of humility in its highest sense:

> Nature understands no jesting; she is always true, always serious, always severe; she is always right, and the errors and faults are always those of man. The man incapable of appreciating her she despises and only to the apt, the pure, and the true, does she resign herself and reveal her secrets.

I have referred to humility as a psychological rather than a religious concept. Many of the leaders and followers of organized religions have exhibited far too much arrogance to be held up as models of humility. Witness the crusades! Or the millions who were slaughtered in central Europe to advance the glory of God![3] Or the present-day advocacy of coercive force from thousands of pulpits to achieve "social goals"! I repeat that the way to freedom is through humility, not arrogance.

---

[3]Father Joseph, a devout Capuchin monk and chief advisor to Cardinal Richelieu, believed that the political ascendency of France was the way to bring God to humanity. For an interesting account of this arrogance—the end justifies the means—see *Grey Eminence* by Aldous Huxley (New York: Harper & Bros., 1941).

Try to imagine a society of know-it-alls, everyone believing himself to be the source of wisdom; all dictocrats, each attempting to dominate all the others. Freedom could not grace such a society—all arrogance, no humility! Indeed, it seems unlikely that such a society could exist. Nature could not reveal any of her secrets to such people; they already know everything. "Blind leaders of the blind."

On the other hand, imagine a population composed mostly of individuals blessed with humility as here defined. Under such circumstances any dictator, or even the least hint of the domineering trait in any person, would be looked upon with disfavor. Demagogues would have no charisma; their siren voices would afford little if any attraction; their schemes to domineer would be ignored. When the domineering trait is curbed, *freedom reigns!* And the process is to acquire and develop the quality of humility!

Finally, there is a thought without which true humility is unattainable: think not of the tyrant as a fool, only of the domineering trait as foolish. It has been wisely said, "Hate not the sinner, only the sin."

3

THE MEEK SHALL INHERIT THE EARTH

Humility, like darkness, reveals the heavenly lights.

—THOREAU

I believe the Third Beatitude has a profound message, perhaps more significant in our time than ever before. Indeed, it may well hold the key to the survival of the human race. If this is so, it behooves us to seek its meaning and to become worthy of its promise.

Seek its meaning? Cannot people as literate as most Americans read plain English? The words, yes; the precise meaning of the ideas those words symbolize, no. Perfect communication presupposes the perfect sayer and the perfect hearer. Which of us is able to say exactly what he means? And what individual accurately hears or reads another's inexactitudes? Approximations at best, even when discoursing in a common language!

Who are "the meek"? Surely not the Casper Milquetoasts —"timid, shrinking, apologetic" persons. It doesn't make sense to suggest that the earth be turned over to them. Yet, this is the image "the meek" first brings to the mind of an English-speaking American. And what is meant by "inherit the earth"? Obviously, it does not mean to ". . . receive (property) by the laws of inheritance." That "the meek shall inherit the earth" must mean far more than it seems. What, pray tell, can it be!

Even a linguistic layman, if he admits the difficulty of communicating in his own language, cannot help but grasp the enormously greater problem in deducing the precise meaning from other languages. There are some simple, concrete words such as yes, *ja, si, oui, da*; but abstract or idea words, more often than not, have no exact equivalent in other languages.

Take the word meek. Originally, it was in Aramaic: *inwethān*. Translated to Greek, it became *praos*. According to the late Gerald Heard,

> There seems little doubt that *praos* stands for a word the meaning of which is opposed to "arrogant," "domineering," "overbearing," "aggressive," "bellicose."

The French translated the Greek *praos* to *debonair*. "That," writes Heard, "is a startling, gay contrast [to meek]. Instead of the motto being 'Please don't kick me,' we find 'Please let me know if there is anything I can do for you.'"

After a careful analysis of the word usage in the period before and during the time of the King James translation, the scholarly Gerald Heard concludes that the word "meek" implied "a wonderful, inherent, teachability."[1] In a word, the Third Beatitude should read, "Blessed are the *teachable* for

---

[1] See *The Code of Christ* by Gerald Heard (New York: Harper & Brothers, 1941), pp. 55-77 and 169-177.

they shall inherit the earth." To my way of thinking, this is wisdom of the highest order.

So, who are the teachable? Today, in the most advanced countries, knowledge—technical, scientific, and the like—is immeasurably greater than, say, twelve decades ago. A few examples:

- Back then we could deliver the human voice at the speed of sound and perhaps a distance of 50 yards. Now? At the speed of light and not only around this earth but far into outer space!
- Human beings then could be delivered at the speed a horse could run. Presently? Around the world in a few hours—even to the moon in a few days!
- My grandfather could bathe in rivers or pools or in rainwater caught in a barrel or cistern or water pumped from a household well. Today? Millions of homes have hot and cold running water often piped from miles away.
- Food? It is no longer confined to what could be raised at home. I enjoy spinach in New York picked the day before in California. The grocery store of my boyhood had no more items than I could rattle off in my head. The store at which I shop today has 10,000 items.

One could go on and on with examples of this miraculous burst of knowledge. In no department of life is the miracle more pronounced than in the harnessing of electrical energy. So dependent have we become on power from this source that a return to twelve decades ago would mean utter collapse. *Hardly anyone doubts that this remarkable economic asset is of our own hands.* Yet, who on earth can define electricity or knows what it is?

What is all of this knowledge doing to modern man? How

does it affect his outlook and his attitudes? The fact that we know how to harness the unknown leads far too many people in today's world to embrace the little god syndrome, convinced that there is no Source above the finite human mind. Infinite though it be, few there are who recognize it. In a recent speech, I repeated the line, "Only God can make a tree." A graduate student sharply responded, "Until now!"

Such arrogance is the very opposite of *inwethān* which the Greeks translated to *praos.* We witness the know-it-alls! Not only are they not teachable but, far worse, they are the authors of authoritarianism and wars. A growing knowledge of how to harness the Unknown, unless scrupulously weighed and put in place, leads to a hopeless separation from the Infinite Unknown—man and Source divorced. This, I suggest, must lead to civil disaster.

So, how are we to describe the teachable, the *inwethan,* the *praos,* the *debonair,* the ones who will "inherit the earth"?

The idea Gerald Heard deduced from *debonair*—"Please let me know what I can do for you"—is not to be overlooked. This comes close to the Golden Rule, and the economics of voluntary exchanges. When I extend kindness and thoughtfulness to you, that is what you will extend to me; likewise when I render services to you in exchange for goods of yours. While such reciprocal relations appear contrary to natural instincts, such mutuality is possible and can be unbelievably rewarding. To prove it, try it!

The teachable are those who have taken the first step in wisdom: acknowledging mystery, they have emptied themselves of know-it-all-ness; humility is their hallmark, wanting-to-know-it-ness their ambition. Bear in mind that no person is educable on any subject prior to a state of inquisitiveness, that is, until his spirit of inquiry is aroused. The teachable are those who are forever probing, who recognize that our earthly gifts are not exclusively of our own hands; they sense that Infinite Something over and beyond their own minds. As seedlings, their roots go down but their shoots shaft toward the heavens. It is the teachable, and they alone, who will "inherit the earth."

What is the meaning of "earth" in this context? In my view, it has nothing to do with acres of diamonds, soil, rock. Rather, it relates to man's earthly potentialities: the evolution or emergence of individual faculties, a growth or development of awareness, perception, consciousness.

Stated another way, those who have so gained a control of themselves as to allow the search for Truth to take charge of their lives, are the ones who have the capacity to live their earthly lives to the full—to whom the *real* treasures of earth belong.

To me the Third Beatitude means simply: *The teachable shall be graced with a realization of their earthly potentialities.* Your or my understanding of and adherence to this wisdom may not "save" the human race but it is the key to one's own salvation—the only commission you and I have been given.

4

LIFE STYLES

We live in deeds, not years, in
thoughts, not breaths; ... He most
lives who thinks most, feels the
noblest, acts the best.

—GAMALIEL BAILEY

Some authors are praised more for their style than for the
content of their work; others are criticized for the lack of
style. According to Longfellow, "With many readers, bril-
liancy of style passes for affluence of thought; they mistake
buttercups in the grass for immeasurable gold mines under-
ground."

There are styles in music ranging from Bach to rock.

Observe how styles have changed in paintings: from communicative art such as Raphael's "The School of Athens" to
the noncommunicative works of Picasso and others of the
"modern school."

Hairdos and dress? How styles have changed from this to
that, to nothing—and back again!

My concern, however, is not so much with changing styles
in dress or art as with swings in thinking for self, nobility
of mind, acting one's best—the changes in style of life. Shifts

17

in life styles appear to be as extreme as those cited above—though perhaps not as easily noted or measured. The question is, are the changes in life style the result of the same type of force as are the changes in dress? Are we dragged from freedom into authoritarianism or lifted from authoritarianism to freedom by the same influences that shift us from communicative to noncommunicative art and back again? If so, we should learn what these forces and influences are.

Perhaps the German poet, Schiller, glimpsed the answer: "Man is an imitative creature, and *whoever is foremost leads the herd.*" Whether the movement is good or bad, upward or downward, there is always someone who is foremost, at the head of the class. The millions, for the most part, are imitators; they follow the leader. As to the style in dresses, for instance, it was not that millions of women simultaneously thought of and adopted mini-skirts. Some designer had a notion and it "caught on." Similarly, it was not that millions of farmers demanded in unison that they be paid for not growing food. A politician or bureaucrat had a "bright idea" which farmers then took to be their "right." Styles of whatever kind are set in this manner.

Parenthetically, styles in all fields appear to deteriorate or improve, to go up and down together—as if in an elevator. We note morality, religion, newscasting, poetry, art, economic thinking, or whatever, ascending or descending as if in a package. For instance, we do not observe statesmanship on the upswing while education is on the downswing. All of history seems to confirm this pattern of relatedness in styles; a renaissance follows the "dark ages"; then a decline, succeeded in turn by an era of progress; and so on. Action, reaction; evolution, devolution!

Be it noted, also, that the masses of people feel as certain of their righteousness when their situation is deteriorating as when it is improving. The millions have no more doubt about their rectitude when they are falling into authoritarianism—slavery—than when they are rising and becoming free and self-responsible. It is imitation in either situation! There is, wrote Van Wyck Brooks, "the illusion that to be modern is worth all the other virtues; . . . as if to keep up with the mode were more important than any of the great realities of life. . . ." Keeping up with the mode or the style is the form of influence that sways the countless millions who do no thinking for themselves.

The solution, if there be one, is to change the life style. But how in heaven's name can this be done? A clue is to be found in this sage observation:

Men, it has been well said, think in herds; it will be seen that they go mad in herds, while they only recover their senses slowly and one by one.[1]

The right course can be pursued only when it is recognized that the recovery of senses is a one-by-one process. Never has there been a massive upward swing in intelligence and righteousness. Rather, we find always the one, the style-setter, the foremost—in combination with the masses of imitators.

Setting the style for the downward swings is as easy as falling off a log: simply refuse to think, practice bad habits, repeat nonsense, cater to weakness and greed. The upward swing, on the other hand, is as difficult as the other is easy.

---

[1] See *Extraordinary Popular Delusions and the Madness of Crowds* by Charles Mackay (New York: Noonday Press, 1969), p. xx. From the Preface to edition of 1852.

Falling is simply "letting yourself go"; rising demands the exercise of every talent and virtue within one's reach. A higher life style calls for the person "who thinks most, feels the noblest, acts the best." The foremost!

Who might that individual be? He might be the one you see in the mirror! True, the countless millions tend to be imitators; yet each of us is *potentially* a style-setter. Every one of us has hidden talents unknown to others—or even to ourselves! The problem is to unmask or release that talent, and this has to be an "inside job."

There is only one way to look at this problem: that person *could* be you or me. In the absence of such a possibility, there can be no style-setter of any account, no one of sufficient magnetism or attractiveness to start the upswing. This is to say that no one is warranted in his rising expectations unless he is preparing himself to serve as exemplar. The matter is far too urgent to "let George do it"; each person is accountable for himself.

So, let anyone who is really concerned reflect on his own solution, namely, unmasking, releasing his hidden talents. But where will he find the formula? I recently stumbled onto an answer and referred to it as "the law of readiness."[2] Original? Hardly! According to an ancient Hindu saying, "When the pupil is *ready,* the teacher will appear." To my way of thinking, that is an important truth and, as Emerson wrote, "The greatest homage we can pay to truth is to use it." Thinking of ourselves as pupils, which doubtless we should, how do we ready ourselves that the teacher may appear? What are the successive steps to becoming a style-setter?

---

[2]See the first three chapters in my book, *Who's Listening?* (Irvington-on-Hudson, N.Y.: The Foundation for Economic Education, Inc., 1973).

To unmask, to release one's hidden talents, seems to require that he become a pupil. Anyone who is unable or unwilling to undertake the effort and joy of learning is well advised to forget the subject here in question, for he seems destined to stay with the herd, the imitators. No teacher ever appears to a know-it-all or to one who cares not.

Who is the teacher that will appear when the pupil is ready? The answer is shrouded in mystery. Might as well ask: from whence comes insight? How explain an intuitive thought? There are forces at work about which we know nothing—except that they are at work! At the moment of readiness, a book will appear, or someone will drop a relevant remark. Indeed, the idea one seeks may come in a dream. The teacher in these instances? Who knows! Edison, Henry Poincare, and ever so many other creative individuals have acknowledged the mystery. They concede that ideas come to them "as if from out of the blue." The "teacher," as the term is used here, is an *enlightenment* regardless of the form in which it shows forth. Does all of this sound unbelievable? Perhaps it is to anyone who has walled himself off from such experiences, but conviction comes when the matter is put to the test. The proof will be disclosed as the effort is made.

Conceded, no two persons achieve readiness in the same way. It appears to be a natural or inherited trait with a few. Observe child prodigies—"to the manner born." They come onto this earth already unmasked; their talents are not hidden. The mill run of us, however, are not thus graced. Nothing short of a disciplined, conscious effort can break down the walls and permit an escape from mediocrity. Here are some of the steps to readiness which have worked to some extent for me.

- The first requirement, as I see it, is nothing less than a passionate, prayerful desire to realize one's potentialities, to tap the resources within. To be unresponsive to this urgency is to spend one's years with the undiscovered self.

- Desire for readiness, by itself, is useless. It's like craving for "all this and heaven too" without striving. Said Franklin, "He that lives on hopes will die fasting." Any realization of the desire must be backed up, accompanied by, indefatigable and joyful effort. If it isn't joyful nothing will happen—the mask won't lift, the teacher will not appear.

- The goal of readiness must have top priority. One eats, sleeps, exercises, earns a living, saves, reads, listens, even chooses conversationists, not as ends in themselves but as means to this noble goal. Otherwise, the promise that "the teacher will appear" is but pretty phrasing, the words of a dreamer.

- Rid the self of distractions that the eye may be focused on the object; get all chores into the past tense pronto! The teacher puts in no appearance amidst shambles, be they on the desk or in the mind. Clear the decks!

- So the mind is barren! What else is there to think through, you say? Confess this plight and make a simple plea for a clue: "If you please." Confess to and ask from whom? The ever-seeking self is sufficient. If the preparations be adequate, the teacher will appear and in short order, as if by magic. "Seek and ye shall find." If in doubt, try it!

- Yes, the teacher will appear announcing the subject to be explored—but just the subject and nothing more. The teacher will go no further—enlightenment will not begin —until the pupil begins. This is to say that the teacher can send no thoughts until the pupil's receiving set is turned on and tuned in. Of what does this machinery consist? Pure and undisturbed concentration on the subject that has been announced! And persistence! Regardless of how dark the outlook or how hopeless the prospects of success, try, try and try again. Presto, the light! Off comes the mask! Behold, the discovered self!

- The technique of trying? Put the ideas on paper; resort to the written word. This makes it possible for the ever-seeking self to capture all that comes to mind and put it in orderly sequence. As each step is spelled out and recorded, the next step becomes obvious.

The above are my steps to readiness, set forth with the hope that, perchance, they might serve another. As Shakespeare said, "Readiness is all." Readiness is indeed all if one aspires to be a style-setter—the foremost. And why not? Is there a nobler earthly goal than this? Why should not everyone spend his years with the world's most important person—the discovered self!

5

SHOEMAKER, STICK TO YOUR LAST

The structuring of a good society is as much your "last" as any other concern.

Before exploring the propriety of this ancient adage, let us enjoy the comedy of its reputed origin. Galileo tells the story:

Apelles was court painter to Alexander the Great. He is reported on one occasion to have stationed himself behind one of his paintings in order to listen to the remarks of the spectators. When a passing shoemaker was heard criticizing the representation of a boot, Apelles stepped out to thank the workman and ask for correction. But the emboldened cobbler then began to extend his adverse remarks to other parts of the picture, and Apelles stopped him with the now proverbial admonition: "Let the shoemaker stick to his last."[1]

---

[1]See *Discoveries and Opinions of Galileo,* translated by Stillman Drake (Garden City, N.Y.: Doubleday Anchor Books, 1957) p.82.

What this admonition amounts to is this: Mind your own business! At first blush, this has all the earmarks of unqualified good counsel. Take my own case: I know substantially nothing about boots, paintings, musical composition, or countless other matters. Far be it from me to tell a cobbler or an Apelles or a Bach what to do. Clearly, there are thousands of ventures, befitting the uniqueness of others, that are beyond my ken and are no business of mine. Apelles was right in admonishing the shoemaker to stick to his last and he would be equally right were he to tell you and me to mind our own business.

But what is our own business? It is conceivable that simple ignorance keeps me unaware of something that properly *is* my business. My business is to fulfill my responsibilities, and laziness may cause me to shirk my rightful obligations. In short, there is more to minding one's own business than first meets the eye, more than just keeping our noses out of other people's business.

There is a matter of transcendent importance that I believe is everybody's business: *the structuring of a good society!* Were we to concentrate on this aspect of our own business as much as we are inclined to meddle in what is surely none of our business, a good society would be a viable prospect. Why all of this emphasis on the good society? It is the environmental prerequisite to individual fulfillment. And that *is* your business—and mine!

The need for a good society is and always has been low on the list of popular human cravings and aspirations. Yet, there is no other subject since the dawn of history about which more has been written. Here is a matter that is everybody's business, but relatively few recognize their responsibility.

The subject is seemingly so difficult that most people pigeon-hole it as one of those specialized activities that is none of one's business—something like the shoemaker telling Apelles how to paint a picture.

Wherein lies the cause of this enigma? Why all of this per-plexity? When people in general are unaware of their per-sonal stake in the good society and have no opinions of their own, when they think this is a matter requiring only the at-tention of specialists, they cannot tell a wise counselor from a charlatan; they are the easy victims of utopian dreamers, seekers after power, organizational gadgetry designers.

Let me venture a guess: the thoughts and ideas that have been written and spoken on the sane and sound side of this subject are as abundant as the plethora of fallacious notions. The former, however, are but little heeded; whereas, millions of people support and applaud the latter. How is this one-sidedness to be explained? People who insist that it is none of their business and who remain intellectually sterile so far as the good society is concerned, are attracted to political gimmicks, to shortcuts, to promises of rewards that put no demands upon them—none whatsoever! All this and heaven too, and no need to attend to personal virtues!

Why do so many people get the false notion that the struc-turing of a good society is over their heads? It is simply be-cause the schemes to which they are attracted—promises of the guaranteed life—are so varied, complex, and nonsensical that no one can understand them, not even the authors! It is not because people are lacking in a capability to understand but, rather, that their eyes are cast upon that which cannot be comprehended. They are not blind; they are simply staring at darkness!

Where then is the light? The light is within the undiscovered self! And the only problem is to find it. If this procedure is simple, then the structuring of the good society is simple; for society, we must remember, is but a name we give to the aggregate of all the *You's* and *I's*. You and I give society whatever character it has, and no society can be better than are the individuals who compose it. You cannot make me good, or even better than I am. Nor can all the social planners and schemers in the world. I alone have any control over my goodness or improvement, and you alone over yours. To become aware of this and then to strive for self-improvement is to mind one's own business—including one's obligation to promote the good society.

How simple is it to become the good citizen? As simple as to understand and to adhere to the most widely pronounced and the oldest ethical proposition of distinctly universal character: the Golden Rule.

There is a companion guideline to good citizenship, as simple to follow and as infallible as the Golden Rule: "Seek ye first the Kingdom of God and His Righteousness, and all these things shall be added unto you." Another way to phrase this guideline is: put truth and righteousness first and foremost, that is, make righteous action one's prime objective, forgetting the things of this world. What happens? The things of this world flow miraculously as a consequence. Caution: Never practice righteousness because of these things which flow as dividends; that puts things first. The result? Neither goodness nor things! Righteousness for the sake of righteousness—period!

From my seat in the bleachers, I judge that these simple guidelines to the improved self and the good society have been seldom used of late. Modern man seems to think that these were only for the poor souls of the ancient world and not for the advanced and the wise such as we! Wiseacres looking down upon the wise—or, so it seems to me.

However, an encouraging change is afoot, and here is one example of it:

> One year ago I went to work for _____ Mutual Life Company. They told me at the time that I would not be a success in the business as I refused to use the selling gimmicks common to the industry. I felt that life insurance in its proper place did have a purpose and that there was room for at least one underwriter that would put the interests of the consumer ahead of his personal gain, the end result being that if I was doing a good job, I would somehow make a living also. The results were much better than expected—I not only made my living, I was the number one producer of life-disability & health insurance in the company for 1972. So I am still of the opinion that honesty pays!

The honesty referred to is precisely the same manner of conduct commended in the ancient guidelines. Heads of auto agencies, brokers, and others are reporting this same approach to me, with results no less astounding than the above. A friend in Tokyo has just sent me a book, *The Matsushita Phenomenon,* revealing that the outstanding industrial success in Japan is on this identical ethical wave length.[2] If numerous instances of this kind come to my attention, I assume there are many that do not; at least, I prefer to believe that an ethical and moral upswing is on its way.

---

[2]See *The Matsushita Phenomenon* by Rowland Gould (Tokyo: The Diamond Publishing Co., Ltd., 1970).

Observe that this movement, now in its initial stage, is strictly voluntary, the only way that man can act in a free market society. And the market is automatically free when government is limited to keeping the peace, that is, to restraining destructive actions. Contrast this with the coercive society manifested by people in all walks of life saying, in effect, "I paid for it; I might as well get my share." Implicit in this latter way of life is dictocratic control of creative activities: "Do as I say, or else!"

When any formula for the good society is not simple, forget it. When any formula cannot be understood by the so-called common man, forget it. Any formula that is not simple is not understood by anyone, even the author.

Keep always in mind the sage counsel of the eminent German psychiatrist, Dr. Fritz Kunkel: "Immense hidden powers lurk in the unconscious of the most common man—indeed, of all people without exception."

With Apelles, we can say "Shoemaker, stick to your last." But the structuring of the good society is as much your "last" as any other concern of yours, regardless of who you are. And in order to mind one's own business this matter must be tied with the improvement of self for first place among our priorities.

6

THE BLESSINGS
OF ADVERSITY

*Adversity has the effect of eliciting
talents which in prosperous circumstances would have lain dormant.*

—HORACE

Many devotees of freedom observe the current plunge into
socialism—state interventionism, welfarism—and lament the
hard times they see ahead. Full of foreboding, they fail to see
that this adversity has its value, its blessings.

Prosperity, as Plutarch reminded us, "puffs up narrow
souls, makes them imagine themselves high and mighty."
When millions of people get this way, as today, they are no
asset to freedom—the "high and mighty" never are. Thus,
freedom loses much of its intellectual sustaining power which
makes easy the plunge into socialism. Only common sense
can come to the rescue, but the adversity can stimulate this
needed quality. For it is an observed fact that the art of becoming consists of acts of overcoming. Without obstacles to
overcome, rising to higher levels is out of the question. The

adversities now facing us may serve as stepping stones; they are blessings in disguise.

We must seek out the vantage point from which to view the present obstacles as necessary stimulants for better thinking —as did Robert Service:

It's a different song when everything's wrong,
When you are feeling infernally mortal;
When it's ten against one, and hope there is none;
Buck up little soldier, and chortle!

Buck up! What does Service mean? He's not telling us to grimly get into the fight, but joyously into the play! It means accenting what's right as distinguished from cursing and berating the wrongdoers and their assertions; it means becoming more productive ourselves. On this point, Goethe observed, "What we agree with leaves us inactive, but contradiction [an obstacle] makes us productive." A personal experience:

My first book was written 36 years ago under the most trying conditions. It was typed in spare moments while traveling extensively over the western states, lecturing to people many of whom were swayed by the statism then on the upswing. For the most part, these were quarrelsome and contentious rather than cooperative audiences.

The book received enthusiastic approval from several persons whose judgment I respected. And then this silly thought: If I could write this well under such adverse conditions, think what I might produce were I not burdened with overwork ·among unfriendly people! Free me from adversity and I would rise to new heights!

With this thought in mind, I took a month off in a cottage

by the seashore. All was beautiful, quiet, serene. No news-
papers or radio; not a soul to bother me; no nonsensical
notions to arouse any rebuttals. The outcome? One month
and nary an idea! I returned to the world of bustle and conflict, with my typewriter and a ream of paper untouched. And
since then, I have remained in this rough and tumble world
of bumping ideas back and forth. Productive? In addition to
numerous other activities, I have had the temerity to pub-
lish 16 books in the intervening period. Score one for Goethe!

But I venture to disagree with the great Goethe on one
point. By using "we" and "us" he suggests that his rule has
universal application. True, Goethe and many others, who
have attained a measure of intellectual manhood, have a live-
ly reaction to notions that contradict freedom—making them
more productive thinkers. The more the nonsense, the better
their performance and the more determined their search for
truth and ways of clear exposition.

However, people by the millions—those lacking understanding, those whose convictions are only "skin deep"—succumb
to the slightest opposition. Let "the other side" become rich
in cliches, bromides, plausibilities and they subside, throw in
the sponge. They go hither and yon as flotsam and jetsam on
a stormy sea. Contradictions serve only to deaden their initiative and diminish their productivity. They are as ineffective, as useless to the advancement of freedom, as "the
high and mighty."

These people are on dead center, unhappy with themselves
and ineffective in the cause of freedom. There is a joy that at-
tends a life which is successfully overcoming obstacles and
adversities; and here are some ways that have helped me
get on the productive track.

1. If puffed up and among "the high and mighty," deflate and escape from that category. The slightest reflection on the contrast between one's accomplishments and the job ahead assures the required humility, the wisdom of knowing how little one knows.

2. If obstacles and contradictory views fail to stimulate productivity—the search for truth and improved expositions—find out why. The mere search for the answer, if sincere, will turn out to be the answer itself, or a large part of it.

3. The next step—a big one—is to probe into the freedom way of life to the point where faith in its efficacy replaces all doubts. Keep going until an awareness dawns of the miraculous market. How tell when this point has been reached? It is reached when one realizes that the free market—each to his own uniqueness and unfettered exchange—possesses a wisdom unimaginably greater than exists in any discrete individual. For instance, grasp the truth that one need not know how mail would be delivered in the absence of force to be absolutely certain that the market would do it ever so much better than anyone can possibly foresee. The evidence is overwhelming but is hidden under cover of things taken for granted. Merely look under the cover.

4. Well begun, half done! The above is the beginning, the construction of the launching pad, the essential preparation for productivity. How far one will orbit cannot be foretold. Productivity in this realm correlates with improved understanding and wisdom and thus offers infinite possibilities. So far as I know, no person, past or present, has more than scratched the surface in making the case for freedom. The need is as great as the potential rewards, and the field is wide open. Enter with joy and enthusiasm.

Any individual, thus prepared, will be stimulated into productivity by socialistic cliches, bromides, plausibilities—contradictions of freedom whether so intended or not. Such an individual will instantly recognize these fallacies and be able to explain the better ideas that ought to displace them. His explanations, then, are productions—blessings of adversity.

Here, for example, are several of the more common fallacies of socialism:

1. "The more complex the society, the more government control we need."
2. "The government should do for the people what the people are unable to do for themselves."
3. "The size of the national debt doesn't matter because we owe it to ourselves."
4. "The free market ignores the poor."
5. "Man is born for cooperation, not for competition."
6. "Human rights are more important than property rights."
7. "Consumers ought to be protected by price controls."
8. "One man's gain is another man's loss."
9. "Rent control protects tenants."
10. "Government should control prices, not people."

This is neither the time nor the place to expose each of these fallacies in detail.[1] I would simply point out that each of these slogans is but a variation of the Marxian motto: "From each according to ability, to each according to need." Each implicitly denies the dignity of the individual, denies that he is self-responsible and self-respecting, denies the prin-

---

[1]Suggested answers to 76 of these popular fallacies appear in *Cliches of Socialism* (Irvington-on-Hudson, N.Y.: Foundation for Economic Education).

ciples of private ownership and voluntary exchange, denies the virtues of open competition and market pricing, and declares that government is better able than we ourselves to manage our respective lives.

There is an unseen aspect to this umbrella of popularly acclaimed governmental protectionism. What such intervention amounts to is a closing of the market, thus depriving each of us—in his dual role of producer and consumer—of the vital information afforded by market prices. Freely fluctuating prices describe the ever-changing conditions of supply and demand. Lacking the knowledge provided by a flexible price structure, no individual and no government official can reasonably judge whether to buy or sell, produce or consume. The free market is a conservation device, and without it a man will waste his own energies as well as all other valuable and scarce resources. Only as these scarce resources, including manpower, are privately owned and controlled through open competition can there be any hope of economic progress and the general alleviation of poverty.

If these are times of great adversity, then surely this is a time for greater faith in freedom. Adversity, rather than doing us in, should strengthen and refine our thinking to the point where we overcome it.

7

APPEAL TO
THE INTELLECT

Every man should use his intellect
... as the lighthouse uses its lamps,
that those afar off on the sea may
see the shining, and learn their way.
—HENRY WARD BEECHER

There are a thousand and one faults responsible for the sorry lack of moral and intellectual progress we decry; even more serious are the evils which cause the devolutionary plunge so apparent to any discerning eye. No one will ever spot all the errors; but let each one that is spotted be held to the light that others may recognize it.

Here is an error that has been bothering me, at once enormous and malicious, a fault so common that it appears, on the surface, to be a virtue. What might this be? It is the tendency to appeal not to the potential intelligence of others but, rather, to play upon, to take advantage of, their weaknesses. The fact that one's potential—the undeveloped capacity in each of us—is incomparably greater than his intelligence may explain the deplorable tendency here in question. For, unless one acts as wisely and conscientiously as he can, the road of least resistance must lead to decadence.

To illustrate: Sales researchers have discovered that a price of $4.95, for instance, gives the impression to most people that the item is more in the $4 than the $5 range. While nearly everyone believes with Ben Franklin that "a penny saved is a penny earned," it is not necessarily a mark of frugality to spend 99 nickels to save one. It may be false economy and bad arithmetic. But such weaknesses are exploited. This explains why an item may be priced at $99.99— 9,999 cents—rather than $100.

"Why," I asked a passenger agent in an airport lounge, "do you advertise a trip to Hawaii for $159.95? Why not $160?" At least he was honest with me: "It fools people; that figure makes it look like a bargain." However, I must not leave the impression that this appeal to ignorance rather than to intelligence is a practice peculiar to business. We find it featured in every field of human activity.

Appeals to weakness are the stock in trade of politicians. What will the people fall for? If it is something-for-nothing, then political platforms will promise delivery.

So-called teachers, economists, clergymen by the tens of thousands stoop as often to such cheap tricks as do labor unions, chambers of commerce, PTA's, and countless other organizations. Find out what weak and thoughtless people will demand, support, cheer, follow—be it consumerism or socialism—and "away we go."

Further, those who deplore this appeal to ignorance are well advised to look in the mirror. Any such widespread error tends to "rub off" on everyone. Is there an identifiable form of immunity to this malady? Yes; merely observe if integrity prevails. If one is saying or writing only that which his highest conscience dictates as truth, then definitely, he is appealing to strength or intellect rather than to weakness. Why this claim?

When one acts with integrity, his eye is not cast on cheers, applause, fame, fortune, profits, and other worldly emoluments. Instead, the pursuit of truth and its accurate reporting commands the individual's attention. Is this to wave aside the things of this world? Hardly! Seek ye first Truth and Righteousness, and these things shall be added unto you.

How, then, are we to reverse course and be rid of this mischievous habit of appealing to weakness? The answer: *appeal to intellect.* No matter with whom one is communicating—whether a customer, student, voter, employee, spouse, child, or other—assume his intelligence. How? By making certain that every utterance—written or oral—accurately reflects the truth as one sees it. And watch the recipient of the message rise to the challenge. To expect and believe in another's intelligence has a drawing power, an attractive or magnetic effect.

To test this conclusion, simply ask yourself: When do I best respond? When someone assumes I am stupid and tries to "pull the wool over my eyes," or when he assumes I am as bright as can be? As the famous psychiatrist, Dr. Fritz Kunkel observed: "Immense hidden powers lurk in the unconscious of the most common man—indeed, of all people without exception." Tap these immense hidden powers by an appeal to intellect. Let integrity feature one's every word and deed.

'What? You expect me to give up the practices that are keeping me in business or in office?"

Frankly, I do. I expect better of those who are now or who

have been appealing to weakness. But when a switch is made, if at all, it will be in response to explanations and demonstrations by a few that an appeal to intellect is the way best to serve one's self-interest. No one can prosper for long— materially, intellectually, morally, spiritually—in a society based on appeals to weakness, be the appeals intentional or not.

Always address our appeals to the other person's intellect. For all you or I know, his hidden or latent powers may be greater than yours or mine. In any case, we will have tried our best, not our worst and, by so doing, will have helped ourselves.

8

AWAIT DISCOVERY

*How poor are they who have no
patience.*

—SHAKESPEARE

Two kinds of improvement are required if we are to renew our
rapidly waning freedom. First, a far better understanding of
the philosophy than any of us has now. We need to develop
a high level expertise in making the case for freedom. Second,
a radical change in tactics; that is, a viable methodology for
advancing freedom in harmony with the philosophy itself.

Of the two, the latter is the more important, and for a
simple reason: If everyone's method for advancing an understanding of freedom were correct, there would be no ideological problem. What, then, is right method? It is concentration on the improvement of self as distinguished from efforts
to set others straight. Clearly, were all people devoted to self-
improvement, *confining their efforts to such exemplary behavior,* there would not be a meddler in society; and without
meddlers there could be no socialism, communism, state interventionism or welfarism, call authoritarianism what you
will. So, first, last, and always, look to the method.

Impatience is a tendency of human nature which frustrates our efforts to advance freedom, causing us to act in ways which repel potential colleagues. If others cannot see what is so clear to us, *make* them see: attack, fight, flaunt our superiority—for time is of the essence!This is the activist approach. How do potential converts react? They run in the other direction; and were I in their shoes, I would too! Why? A person uncommitted to a philosophy cannot appreciate its being shouted at him from the housetops. If that's an example of freedom, heaven forbid; I want none of it!

Other obstacles to the attainment of our ideas include (1) the unawareness of an easily demonstrable fact, and (2) a blindness to a promise that can and should be fulfilled.

The fact is this: No one, however skilled, can insinuate or ram an idea into the consciousness of another. This is so because each individual is in charge of his own doors of perception; each admits only what he chooses, and no more. If I could plant my ideas in your mind—make you into my image—you and others could do the same to me, however perfect or deformed the model. We should be grateful that each man is in charge of his own inner sanctum. True, there are some copycats or hero worshipers who ape their idols and echo other men's words. But they do not possess the ideas to the point of acting upon them; they give off only shallow repetition and mimicry. Never count an imitator as a soul won to freedom or to any other way of life. All attempts to bring others to our point of view by pressure tactics, no matter how well intentioned, are destined to fail; they do not good but harm!

Now to the promise that can and should be fulfilled: If you or I or anyone else has one or more ideas or truths or bits of wisdom that are worthy of another's possession, *let that other discover this gold mine for himself.* Do I mean that one should not advertise his intellectual prowess; that he should wave no flags calling attention to his expertise, remain silent until asked? Precisely! Do absolutely nothing beyond the improvement of self, that is, the building and stocking of one's own storehouse!

The promise that can be trusted: If you or I have anything another believes to be worth taking, he will find us out by himself, knock at our doors, and ask our counsel. Incredible? To most people, yes. But look to history for confirmation. Who are the persons over the past three thousand years whose wisdom was sought during their lifetimes and is sought unto this day? They are the ones who perfected their own grasp of truth, not those who merely displayed themselves. Neither Socrates nor any of these wise men attempted to ram their ideas into people's heads; not only their contemporaries, but many persons in subsequent centuries, discovered them and sought their tutorship. Or, if the historical record fails to convince, then look to yourself. From what person, from what sources, do you seek guidance? An inventory will be both surprising and instructive.

At work here is a universal law—the Law of Attraction. Excellence exerts an invisible magnetic force upon those who seek it. Indeed, anyone graced by excellence cannot help being discovered. There is no way for him to hide his light under a bushel—unless he refuses to share when asked. And no person of excellence could do such a thing; he has, by definition, risen above such meanness.

We know from experience that animals are drawn to those who love them and are repelled by hate or indifference. Science is now revealing that this same principle of attraction and repulsion applies even to plant life. Likewise, human beings are drawn to persons of excellence and are repelled by domineering show-offs. And this is the way it should be.

There remains, however, the most compelling reason why no one of us should parade his "wisdom," but rather await discovery. *It is only when a person has discovered a bit of enlightenment for himself that he really possesses it.* Self-discovery and self-possession are inseparably linked. "Seek and ye shall find" has a logical extension: What ye find shall be thine.

The inspiration for this chapter came at a recent FEE Seminar in Utah. A young man had traveled hundreds of miles to attend. Rarely have I come upon a person so quick and eager to learn the freedom philosophy. Why his exceptional interest? When I asked, he explained how he had quite inadvertently discovered FEE and the philosophy which we try earnestly to improve. He had now made these ideas his own because he himself had made the discovery. We had never tried to "reach" him; he reached for us.

On my return from Utah, a letter informed me of another discoverer:

> My good friend, Dave, is more pleased with his discovery of FEE than if he had discovered oil in his backyard!

With my attention focused on these two experiences, I became suddenly aware of countless cases no less impressive—plain, convincing instructions to await discovery.

When we hurl or shout our know-it-all-ness at others, the impact sends them away from, not toward, the free society. The "wisdom" bounces back in the direction from whence it came and is never possessed by the persons at whom we aimed it. All loss and no gain! On the other hand, any person who discovers a bit of light on his own initiative is truly enlightened because he made the discovery.

Finally, what is my role? Who, among all the world's people, is my major concern? Myself! Not you, and not anyone else, simply because others are beyond my powers to correct. Nor must my motivation for self-improvement be as a means toward your improvement or anyone else's—only my own. To the extent that I succeed, to that extent *may* some of my enlightenment be discovered. But that is up to others, not me.

Imagine that a considerable number of individuals were to take this approach. Enlightenment—the overall luminosity— would be ever so much greater than now. Why? Because each would then be brightening his own candle—the only one over which he has any control.

Await discovery! Simply make certain that, if and when another seeks your light, it is as bright as it can be.

9

SAY WHAT YOU MEAN

You can reflect what is another's;
You can radiate only what is your
own.

—CHINESE PROVERB

Recently I remarked to my long-time and most intimate acquaintance, "You know, it has been dawning on me that nearly everything I have written for the past 25 years is the same old theme song—only the titles are different!" The reply, "I have known that all the time!" It is not merely that I am slow to catch on; it is more a case of trying to follow the counsel of a wise friend of my earlier days, "Say what you mean and mean what you say."

To mean what you say is properly labeled as integrity: the accurate reflection in word and deed of whatever one believes to be right. Anyone who so wills it can do this. No need to belabor this point.

But saying what one really means, even on a single theme, is a goal without end, that is, if the thought is growing, expanding, becoming more meaningful. Further, there are endless ways of saying what one means and in each new way there is some enlightenment—for self if not for others. For in-

45

stance, have you not tried over and over again to explain an idea to a person, his only response being a blank stare? And then, finally, there is the right phrasing for this person and his face lights up: "I *now* see what you mean!" As W. E. Hickson phrased it, "If at first you don't succeed, try, try, try again."

My main theme, for lo these many years? *The sole way to a better world is the improvement of self as distinguished from the reforming of others.* Few, indeed, are those who have responded, "I see what you mean." But now there comes to my attention the ancient Chinese Proverb which makes precisely the same pronouncement, except in different and doubtless better phrasing than I have ever contrived: one can reflect what is another's; one can radiate *only* what is his own. An excuse for my theme under still another title!

To "reflect," as meant in this Proverb, is only to echo what one reads or hears; it is not of the self and, thus, has no communicative muscle; it is as powerless as one's own reflection in the mirror. Many, if not most, of the words that are spoken and written today fall in this useless category; they are as meaningless as a prayer by rote, that is, they are without understanding or thought—as unattractive as a broken record!

True, to reflect in the mockingbird sense, saying what others said by rote, is but babble. One must not, however, gloss over that other kind of reflection which is quite the opposite, reflection that accounts for all intellectual, moral, and spiritual acquisition, the sole fountain of radiation. Coleridge puts this idea in focus:

> There is one art of which every man should be a master—the art of reflection. If you are not a thinking man, to what purpose are you a man at all?

On this matter of reflection and radiation, we must bear in mind that the individual is at once a receiving and broadcasting station; he can radiate only that which has first been received, that is, made his own. This is to say that his broadcasting range is limited by the extent and depth of his reflections—by how good a thinking man he is.

I am reminded of a time—1910—long before TV and even radio, when I built a wireless receiver and transmitter. While mounted on the same box, the receiving and sending parts were unrelated. This gadget could receive from a distance of 500 miles, but could transmit no more than two miles. As distinguished from a human being, these two parts had nothing to do with each other. We humans, for the most part, resemble that boyhood wireless in a single respect: our reception usually encompasses a greater range than does our broadcasting. At least, I find this to be the case.

To repeat, a person can radiate only that which has first been received, reflected upon, digested, made his own! Thus, no one but a thinking man can radiate.

What does the thinking man think about? Reflect upon? He contemplates radiations—in the form of ideas! From whence come these? They stem from two sources: the Voice Within and the Voices Without, each being a form of radiant energy.

As Emerson said, "We lie in the lap of an immense intelligence." This, as all radiant energy, is a flowing phenomenon; it flows through all life—constantly!

The Voice Within is that part of this intelligence which one personally succeeds in intercepting: tiny flashes of enlightenment referred to as insight, intuition, discovery, invention, creativity. Whatever is intercepted becomes one's own. An idea successfully intercepted can, in turn, be radiated; that which has been received may be transmitted, although transmittal is difficult and requires considerable skill.

All intelligence at the human level originated with this Voice Within—yours, mine, or someone else's.

As to the Voices Without, countless persons have, since the dawn of consciousness, intercepted bits of this "immense intelligence," making these bits of wisdom their own. Their enlightenments are, more or less, in radiation. The thinking man tries to tune these into his receiving set, making them, as well as the Voice Within, his own.

Finally, is it really true that one can radiate only that which is his own?

My answer is an unequivocal *yes!* Why then are there so few persons who will accept this axiom as a guiding thought? It is simply this: most of us have intercepted so little of the "immense intelligence"—made it our own—that we have nothing to radiate. When this is the case, it is extremely difficult to acknowledge as valid those phenomena which lie beyond one's own experiences.

Obviously, no one can radiate mental energy or thought that has not been intercepted, received. Broadcasting or radiating creative thought—phases of the "immense intelligence" —is governed by the tuning-in range of one's receiving set and the power of his amplifier. If one is radiating nothing, then let him draw the self-evident and unhappy conclusion and set about its correction: the perfection of self—striving to become a better thinking man.

To whom does this corrective process apply? To every living person—without exception!

10

THE CONFESSION
OF ERROR

*To make no mistake is not in the
power of man; but from their errors
and mistakes the wise and good
learn wisdom for the future.*

—PLUTARCH

Many people, I suspect, would rather entitle this chapter "the error of confession" than "the confession of error."

My thesis is that error can and should play a profound role in man's advancement toward wisdom. There are two doors through which the fallible individual must pass before he can behold the light of truth. The first is the discernment of error; the second is the *confession of the error,* not only to self but to anyone influenced by his error, whether that influence extend to one or to a few or to millions of persons. Rarely does the individual err in solitude; most of one's mistakes have a social impact, may indeed bring harm to others as well as to himself. So, one is socially obligated to confess as well as to correct his errors.

A personal experience may help illustrate my point. In 1945 I was given the assignment of choosing two speakers to pre-

Often the explanation of our error is made by a political opponent or by one having a faith or general philosophy we do not approve, that is, by our "enemies"—persons we abhor or, at least, do not like. The very source is enough to close our eyes and mind; we will have none of it! Indeed, this lack of catholicity on the part of anyone tends to confirm him in the rightness of his mistaken views. Small chance of confessing errors thus buried in rancor!

The fact that society, today, is in one of those devolutionary swings—common to history—and that countless people are proposing remedies of every variety and without success, suggests that the right answer has not yet been found.

I venture to say that the remedy is simple; indeed, if it is not simple, in all probability it is not right. The first step is to *remove all obstructions to the discernment of error; and the second is to confess the mistake openly.* How wonderfully different would be the societal situation were a considerable number of us to open these two doors. It seems obvious to me that this is the way and the only way to wisdom, truth, light!

A considerable number! Yes, but a number of individuals, one by one. After all, it is not society that acts; it is only discrete human beings.

There is no point in dwelling further on removing the obstructions to the discernment of error. Count him out who cannot rid himself of prejudice, bias, egotism, know-it-all-ness. Include only those who welcome exposure of error, regardless of source.

The door most of us have had no practice in opening is the second: open confession of discerned error, not only to self but to all who have come under the harmful influence of the mistake. By "open confession," I am not referring to any maudlin wailing. Rather, I am talking about a clear explanation of one's new insight—the truth that displaces the error he had espoused and inflicted on others as well.

There are two points to keep in mind. First, if the purpose of life is to grow in awareness, perception, consciousness, the refusal to confess error is to strangle growth; it is to nail one's self down to mediocrity, along with others under influence of one's errors. Be free!

Second, confession not only is good for the soul; it also turns out to be a joyous experience, as is any freedom from inhibitions. To prove it, try it!

11

PENALTY OF SURRENDER

*It is by compromise that human
rights have been abandoned. The
country . . . deserves repose. And
repose can only be found in ever-
lasting principles.*

—CHARLES SUMNER

A certain business leader, perhaps among the most publicized
during the last two decades, once severely lectured me on my
unswerving and uncompromising behavior. He charged that I
saw things only in blacks and whites. He argued that practical
life was lived in shades of grays, actually in the shadows of
these two extremes. He suggested that I had a nice chance
of "going far" in the world, if only I would become more
pliable to the thoughts and actions of my fellows. He really
wanted me to be more agreeable to his middle-of-the-road
political theories.

The compromising attitude is exalted by many and deplored by only a few. Most current discussions are tempered
with concepts of compromise and expediency.

Compromise, like many other words, has different meanings for different persons. I want to use the term in the sense
of one of the definitions given by Webster: "The result or em-

bodiment of concession or adjustment." I wish to show that compromise is potentially good when applied in a physical sense and that it has no application whatever in a moral sense.

For example, you and your wife are spending what is hoped will be a happy evening at home. She chooses to watch TV and you elect to explore Mises' *Human Action*. The scene appears peaceful as you sit side by side near this piece of furniture. But to you the furniture is making a lot of distracting noise.

Here are all the possibilities for turning a cheerful evening into one of disharmony. But compromise can come to your aid. Your wife can decrease the noise of the TV to the point where she can still hear it, and you can move to some remote corner where you can comprehend Mises just as well as anywhere else. Harmony can thus be preserved by compromise.

Compromise in this sense is an adjustment of physical situations. It is the process by which conflicts are reduced to the point most satisfactory to all parties concerned. When thought of in this way, compromise is the great harmonizer, the attitude that makes living together—social life—a pleasure.

Indeed, the market place of willing exchange where tens of millions of transactions go on daily is one vast area of compromise. Buyers aim at low prices. Sellers aim at high prices. In a free market, unhampered by private thieves and political restrictions, there is an adjustment of these diverse desires. Compromise establishes the price at which the mutual satisfaction of buyer and seller is at its highest level.

It is in the physical realm that most of our daily life is lived. In this realm compromise is good and it is practical. It begets harmony and peace.

How easy it would seem then, finding compromise so useful in such a vast segment of life, to conclude thoughtlessly that it has an equal place, a comparable value, in that phase of life which consciously occupies little of our thoughts: moral life.

But this is precisely the point where I believe many of us are the victims of a confusion of terms. What is compromise in physical affairs—that is, in an adjustment of physical positions—is something entirely different when applied to principles and morality.

For example, let us make the reckless assumption that most of us are committed to the Biblical injunction, "Thou shalt not steal." This is based on the moral principle that each person has the right to the fruits of his own labor. The point I wish to make—my major point—is that this *as a principle* defies compromise. You either take someone else's property without his consent, or you do not. If you steal just a bit—a penny—you do not compromise the principle; you abandon it. You surrender your principle.

By taking only a *little* of someone's property without his consent, as distinguished from taking a lot, you do compromise in the physical sense the amount you steal. But the moral principle, whatever the amount of the theft, is surrendered and utterly abandoned.

If all the rest of mankind is in favor of passing a law that would take the property, honestly acquired, of only one person against his will, even though the purpose be allegedly for the so-called social good, I cannot adjust myself both to the moral injunction, "Thou shalt not steal," and to the demand of the millions. Principle does not lend itself to bending or to compromising. It stands impregnable. I must either

abide by it, or in all fairness, I must on this point regard myself as an inconsistent, unprincipled person rather than a rational, reasonable, logical one.

The question immediately arises as to what constitutes
principle. Here again is a term with varying meanings to different persons. I must, therefore, define what I mean.

The Ten Commandments are admonitions derived from the
religious experience of an ancient people. In terms of their
origin, the Commandments are cast in the form of intercepts
of the will of God; in terms of their application, they are im-
peratives admitting of no dilution. They were expressions of
principles at least to the ones who received them, and have
been adopted as such by countless millions. Their acceptance springs from the studied deductions of the wiser among
us, confirmed through centuries of observation and experience.

The correctness of a principle has little to do with the intensity of conviction with which a man holds it. Someone
else may hold a contrary principle with like intensity. No man
can get nearer to the truth than his own highest apprehension
of it. Ultimate insights may differ, and such differences will
always be part of the human scene. But there is another type
of difference which is more pertinent to the point of this es-
say: the difference between those who accept unyieldingly
a moral principle as their standard, and those who accept a
principle watered down by "practical" considerations. Lord
Morley warned of this danger when he deplored the tendency
to forget the principle itself in our preoccupation with the
practical difficulties of applying it.

To me, "Thou shalt not steal," is a principled injunction,
not alone because some sage of antiquity said so, but largely

because my own experience has compelled me to adopt this as a principle of right conduct which must be adhered to if I am not to destroy my own integrity, and if I am to live peacefully with my fellow men.

To those of opposite judgments, who believe that they should gratify their personal charitable instincts not with their own goods, but with goods extorted from others by the police force, who fail to see how thieving damages integrity, and who accept the practice of political plunder as right and honorable—to them, "Thou shalt not steal" must appear wrong in principle.

Whether a principle is right or wrong cannot in any ultimate or absolute sense be determined by any single one of us human beings. Principles on the level of human perception are what are judged to be the rules of life or nature; what are judged to be universal, eternal verities; what are judged to be fundamental points of reference. But human judgment is fallible. Therefore, whether a stated principle is held to be right or wrong will depend on the quality of the individual's judgment. Aristotle claimed that there were a million ways to be wrong; only one way to be right. How easy for fallible beings to decide on a wrong way!

Sound judgment leads toward right principles. No person can rise above his best judgment, and he can rise only as fast as his judgment improves. On what, then, is an improving judgment dependent? My answer is: on revelation—"The disclosing or discovering . . . of what was before unknown. . . ." Other terms for revelation are insight, cognition, inspiration, extrasensory perception. On what does revelation or insight rest? Surely, on conscious effort, education, the kind of persons with whom one associates, the topics selected for discussion, what one chooses to read—all of these relate to one's perception. More fundamental, however, than anything else is intellectual integrity, without which, I am certain, the cognitive stream cannot flow at its best. Goethe's views, already cited in Chapter 2, bear repeating:

> Nature understands no jesting; she is always true, always serious, always severe; she is always right, and the errors and faults are always those of man. The man incapable of appreciating her, she despises; and only to the apt, the pure, and the true, does she resign herself, and reveal her secrets.

Intellectual integrity simply means to reflect in word and in deed, always and accurately, that which one believes to be right. Integrity cannot be compromised. It is either practiced or not practiced.

Certainly, there is nothing new about the efficacy of accurately reflecting what one believes to be right. This principle of conduct has been known throughout recorded history. Now and then it has been expressed beautifully and simply. Shakespeare enunciated the principle when he had Polonius say:

> This above all: To thine own self be true,
> And it must follow, as the night the day,
> Thou canst not then be false to any man.

Edmond Rostand had the same principle in mind when he wrote for Cyrano:

> Never to make a line I have not heard in my own heart.

The Bible announces the penalty of surrender—what it means to abandon the truth as one sees it:

The wages of sin is death.

Whether the wages of sin be mere physical death, as when men shoot each other over ideological differences, or profound spiritual death, as in the extinction of integrity, character, and self-respect, one needs to make but casual inquiry to verify the rightness of this Biblical pronouncement. Abundant testimony is being provided in our time. Nor is the end in sight.

All the world is filled with examples of surrendered principles: men who know practically nothing about themselves trying to play God, attempting to control and forcibly direct the creative actions of others; the glamour of popularity and shallow earthly fame rather than the concepts of rightness directing the policies of nations; expediency substituting for the dictates of conscience; businessmen employing "experts" to help them *seem* right, often at the expense of rightness itself; labor leaders justifying any action that gratifies their lust for power; political leaders operating on the premise that the end justifies the means; clergymen preaching expropriation of property without consent in the name of the "common good"; teachers not explaining but advocating coercive collectivism; aspirants to public office building platforms from public opinion polls; farmers, miners, and other plunderbundists uniting with the police force to siphon unto themselves the fruits of others' labor; arrogance replacing humility; in short, surrender of principle appears to be the distinguishing mark of our time.

If we were suddenly to find foreign vandals invading our shores, vandals that would kill our children, rape our women, and pilfer our industry, every last man of us would rise in arms.

Yet, these ideas born of surrendered principles are the most dangerous vandals known to man. Is the Bible right that the wages of sin is death? Observe the growth of domestic violence. Note the extent to which the organized police force—government—promotes and enacts plunder rather than inhibits it. Scan the last sixty years of war, hot and cold; wars to end wars, each serving only as a prelude to larger wars. And, today, we worldlings, in angry and hateful moods, stand tense and poised to strike out at each other, not with shillelaghs, pistols, hand grenades and cannons, but with mass exterminators of the germ and atom types, types that only a people of surrendered principles could concoct.

Perhaps it is timidity that prevents many a man from standing squarely on his own philosophy and uttering nothing less than the highest truth he perceives. He fears the loss of friends or position. Actually, the danger lies in the other direction, in settling for less than one's best judgment.

Does it take courage to be honest? Does one have to be brave to express the truth as he sees it? Indeed, *it is not dangerous to be honest,* but rather a mark of intelligence. Being honest and adhering to principle requires intelligence more than courage. Courage without intelligence makes men blusterous and cantankerous with their views; they offend with their honesty. But, the villainy in that case is their cantankerousness, not their integrity.

Finally, some may contend that even if everyone were a model of intellectual integrity, by reason of the great variety of judgments, differences would still remain. This is true. But differences lead in the direction of truth in an atmosphere of honesty. Honest differences are livable differences.

Life in a physical sense is a compromise, a fact that need

not concern us. But when vast numbers of people surrender living by what they believe to be right, it follows that they must then live by what they believe to be wrong. No more destructive tendency can be imagined.

Honesty—each person true to his highest conscience—is the condition from which revelation springs; from which knowledge expands; from which intelligence grows; from which judgments improve. It is a never-ending, eternally challenging—a thoroughly joyous—process. Indeed, it *is* living in its highest sense.

12

WORSHIP, A SINGULAR THING

If we begin by overrating the being
we love, we shall end by treating it
with wholesale injustice.
—**HENRI-FREDERIC AMIEL**

During the early days of FEE several of us observed numerous devotees of the freedom philosophy who had but a single standard for gauging truth: would the man they worshiped— admittedly outstanding—agree or not. If their hero said yes, true; if no, false.

This tendency on the part of ever so many people to worship—genuflect before—another human being, regardless of relative genius, inspired the late Dr. F. A. Harper and me to prepare the following motto which for years has had a prominent place in our FEE workshop:

Seekers after Truth should not be bound by *who* sponsors any idea—Truth being its own witness.

In short, there is no place for idolatry in the freedom philosophy. Previous to learning my lesson the hard way, I received with pleasure anyone's overrated appraisal of me. "I am your disciple," or words to that effect. Then the rude awakening: every instance of overesteem sooner or later turned sour, that is, to rejection. Over the years, many have come and gone—"bosom buddies" to disparagers. Here is a two-sided lesson: never worship or overrate any human being past or present; hope that no other person will ever worship or overrate one's self. No man can really worship many gods; *worship is a singular thing!*

By definition it is singular, for we can accord supreme homage to one object only. Therefore, the single thing that merits worship is Truth—the love and pursuit of it. Call Truth what you will: Infinite Consciousness, Infinite Intelligence, the Infinite Unknown, God. Thus, when one accords omniscience to human beings, he is looking upon them as "having infinite knowledge, knowing all things." This, of course, is absurd. No person, regardless of how ingenious he may be relative to the rest of us, rises above the finite; he knows next to nothing of the Universal Laws; indeed, very little about any one of them. In a word, worship cannot logically be extended to any one or to any number of finite minds but only to the one Infinite Mind.

Support for the contention that no human being has ever known very much may be found in reading *Treasury of Philosophy,* a summary of the views and ideas of the world's most famous philosophers—some four hundred of them.[1] While their philosophical positions are not necessarily antagonistic, no two philosophers are anywhere near identical. All have probed the unknown and returned with what, at

---

[1] See *Treasury of Philosophy,* edited by Dagobert D. Runes (New York: The Philosophical Library, Inc., 1955).

best, are but tiny findings. The only quality these philosophers have in common is variation—one picks up a flicker here, another detects a glimmer there. Not a one has come up with the Whole Truth, and none ever will!

Our own daily experience also supports this claim. No two of us see or hear alike. Indeed, no one of us sees or hears alike from one moment to another. Here, however, is the clincher: anyone who is growing in understanding discovers that the more he knows the more he knows he does not know; the more Truth he discerns, the more humble he becomes. The exploration of the Infinite by finite minds makes this inevitable. Socrates, perhaps the wisest of all, knew he knew nothing; the know-it-all, on the other hand, simply is unaware of how ignorant he is.

When one realizes how near to a know-nothing everyone is, it then becomes clear why overrating another is more than likely to lead, eventually, to "wholesale injustice."

We must understand that our heroes are fallible, too. Otherwise, when one comes upon an articulate person whose beliefs more or less accord with his own, but who possesses the ability to phrase them brilliantly, the tendency is to put that person on a pedestal. "You have put to words what I have always believed." The magnification of one's own tiny light is the cause of this; hero worship is the temporary consequence.

Sooner or later, by reason of the congenital variations existing in the hero and the "worshiper," the latter beholds flaws and errors in the former. Not only does the hero fall from grace; in the eyes of his beholder, he falls on his face! The god turns to dust because he was mistakenly presumed to be a god in the first place.

"You have put to words what I have always believed." Thousands of individuals over the ages have done this for me. However, there are few of these philosophers with whom I completely agree. Great as they are—objects of my admiration and esteem—nonetheless, I have fault to find with Plato, Aristotle, Epictetus, Spinoza, Adam Smith, Goethe, Bastiat, to name but a few. And the same goes for any number of my remarkable contemporaries. Yet, the thoughts and works of these notables I count among my blessings; they have given me countless enlightenments I could never have come upon by myself. Further, they do not fall into disrepute by reason of our differences. Why? I know that they also are fallible human beings, finite minds, even as you and I, probing the Infinite. The fact that I have not regarded any one of them as a god in the first place is the reason why I do not disparage them now. They are my benefactors!

Plato, for instance, instead of being the object of my contempt because he advanced the philosopher-king idea, has my admiration for the thousand and one enlightenments he passed on to mankind, among whom I am a beneficiary. If I do not overrate his strength, I need not disparage a weakness; I can level off at friendship.

By the same token, I hope that no person shall ever overrate me for, should he do so, friendship is doomed, mutual helpfulness at an end.

However, your overrating of others or their overrating of you is tied for second place when it comes to this worshiping error. In first place—by far—is the overrating of self. It is this that spawns the big I AM's and the little Hitlers, the know-it-alls. Tiny specks in the Cosmic Plan posing as Infinite Intelligence! Self-worship to the point where they believe they can direct your life better than you can! Tragic, yes; but comical, nonetheless!

Finally, freedom is impossible in a society overburdened with overraters—either of others or of themselves. When many are know-it-alls, or are overrated as such, freedom of choice is out of the question.

Once the idea is grasped that all persons who have lived upon this earth have experienced no more than tiny glimpses of Truth and that no two perceptions are or ever have been identical, then a great Truth emerges: freedom! Let these ideas freely flow, one from another. Then each person becomes the beneficiary of them all, each graced by the overall luminosity, that is, each blessed with as much wisdom as exists. Viewed in this manner, freedom is the uninterrupted interchange of ideas and goods and services among individuals who worship neither themselves nor one another. Freedom flows in the absence of "big shots"; freedom springs from humility.

Worship, indeed, is a singular thing. Keep it singular and enjoy the blessings of freedom!

13

THE FEAR OF FREEDOM

To love righteousness or intel-
ligence or outstanding talent or
virtue of any sort is to love freedom.

Nearly everyone says he favors freedom, but in reality—with few exceptions in today's world—most people are "scared to death" of it. This ambivalence is not widely recognized, but it is the same thing as the fear of righteousness or intelligence or outstanding talent or virtue of any sort.

However, merely to use the word freedom communicates nothing. No two persons ascribe precisely the same meaning to it; indeed, each individual, as he thinks about freedom, may experience shifting definitions. This word, as are ever so many other terms, is shrouded in fuzziness. So, let me define the freedom to which I refer.

I wish to be free from dictators—all of them—be they of the one-man variety or an agglomeration hiding behind an act of Congress or an administrative ruling that restrains creative actions. Leave me free to do anything I please—stupid or brilliant—so long as it is peaceful and not injurious to others. Let me work at whatever I please for whatever I can obtain by willing exchange, whether the wage be a mere trifle or a king's ransom. Let my hours of labor range as I please from zero to 168 per week—subject, of course, to contracts. And leave me free to exchange whatever I please with whomever I choose, be it with General Electric, Matsushita, or Joe Doakes. Free me from those people who would attend to my welfare, not with the fruits of their own labor in the voluntary practice of charity, but with the coercively exacted income of others. My welfare is no one else's business; it is a matter between me and my God, not between those who levy and those who pay taxes. Finally, free me from fraud, violence, misrepresentation, thievery—the destructive actions of men— the curbing of which is the sole role I would assign to government.

These aspirations, strung together, are what I mean by the kind of freedom of which people are "scared to death"!

Why scared? Gilbert Chesterton once remarked: "It is not that Christianity has been tried and found wanting; it is that it has been tried and found difficult and abandoned." So it is with those who try freedom; they find that it requires responsibility for self. And in consequence of that discovery, belief and faith in freedom is all but abandoned in America today! I emphasize "belief and faith." Were the practice of freedom totally abandoned, all would perish. Freedom is still practiced to a marked extent despite all the barriers, but must wane and disappear eventually without a belief and faith to sustain it.

Stephen Vincent Benét has put our problem in realistic perspective:

Just as a physical fever may be beneficial for its cathartic effect in burning away the poisonous pollutants in the system, even while it is resisted for its painfulness, so freedom may be both sought after and opposed, for we may wish to partake of its benefits *without accepting the burden of its consequences.* (Italics added)

In order rationally to embrace freedom rather than fear it, we must see and understand the two faces of freedom: benefits and burden. If we wish to enjoy the benefits we must accept the burden.

Everyone wishes to partake of the benefits of freedom, its spiritual advantages and its material windfalls. These goods flow *exclusively* from people acting creatively as they choose. The range in benefits is staggering: on the one hand, a loner in an attic is unmolested as he pens a new system of philosophy or paints a masterpiece; on the other hand, an abundance of goods and services is at the beck and call of ordinary people in exchange for such minor performances as writing, lecturing, or hammering nails into a building. It is almost impossible to imagine the countless conveniences one can obtain in exchange for his own specialized output.

Here, however, is the rub: only a minority have the slightest idea that these benefits spring from the unfettered release of creative energy, and even fewer know how to achieve that release. Such failure may be traced to the fallacy of the False Cause: because the muscle of freedom is so strong that the benefits continue to flow from the economy despite increasing political interventions, it is all too easy to assume that the interventions cause the benefits! Many people fall into this trap; they fail to see that government is not the source of productivity but first must seize from producers any goods that it may eventually give to others.

That benefits spring from interventions is a falsity broadcast from every conceivable station: public media, pulpits, classrooms, the halls of Congress—from labor organizers to Lords of Parliament:

> Tired old theories and slogans are trotted out as startling novelties. Bold experiments are proposed in one country that have been repeatedly tested in another. Arguments and counter-arguments are put forth as if their proponents stood in the dawn of history.[1]

Goods and services flow *exclusively* from individuals acting creatively and cooperatively as they personally choose. This is a fact of life, however difficult to grasp: *Freedom affords the only way to release the creativity of the individual.* Contrast this with the opposing formula, coercive regimentation, the dictocrat's method currently on the upswing. Instead of release, it applies restraint! Take any one of countless interventions and examine first its source and next its impact on you.

What is the source? The fountainhead of interventionism is in the process that causes a person to so overestimate his own wisdom and to so belittle yours that he believes he can run your life better than you can. Not even to Solomon would you voluntarily delegate such power, and certainly not to anyone lower on the intelligence scale, that is, to anyone eager to dictate what you produce or exchange or how your tastes should be modified to fit his ever-varying dreams of Shangri-La.

Next, how do these restraints affect you and me? Applied

---

[1]See "The 'Arithmetic of Happiness' Doesn't Add Up" by Peter L. Berger *(Fortune,* October 1972) p. 151.

100 per cent, the restraints would fully paralyze; but to the extent of their application, to that extent are we kept from becoming our creative selves. What part of our property and our earnings belongs to us is their decision, not ours. The hours we shall labor, with whom we shall exchange and at what rates, even our educational efforts are less and less self-determined. Carried a little further and there will be a limit on the thoughts we are allowed openly to express. Let there be widespread surrender to this politico-economic heresy and the individual is no longer a man but a mere statistic.

Let me rephrase my answer to the question: Why is it that so many people believe that our unprecedented and enormous benefits flow from the dictocratic arrangement presently in vogue?

There is indeed a myriad of political controls on the economy, but there is widespread evasion of the controls—a zigzagging around the stoppages of creative action! Creative energy goes coursing through loopholes, no dictocrat nor any combination of them being smart enough to foresee and to block all the ways of possible circumvention. Look about you for abundant evidence, perhaps even in the mirror. In a word, the zest to be a man rather than a statistic, the pull or push of freedom, the will to stay alive, is not easy to down. Just as lightning cuts its own path, so creativity—a form of radiant energy—finds a way.

But reflect on the price for this short-term victory over the political obstacle course: destruction of character! Men, under these circumstances, become schemers. When the dictocratic trend advances far enough—as in England following the Napoleonic Wars—many citizens turn into outlaws, smugglers, black marketeers, breakers of the law. We witnessed many examples of this during World War II under the dicto-cratic price and production controls. What, then, is the price of interventionism? Banditry, a depraved way of life, is sub-stituted for the way of the Golden Rule that characterizes a truly free people.

Yes, the enormous benefits of trade continue for a while in spite of the interventions. Meanwhile, the best and most re-sponsible individuals—creative men—gradually lose their moral character; society slowly disintegrates at the core. This is the dreadful price we pay!

Enough about the one face of freedom—the benefits. But what about the other face—the burden of self-responsibility that "scares people to death"?

Our forefathers escaped from dictocratic arrangements and set up house in a truly underdeveloped country. They were at once free and self-responsible, neither condition being pos-sible without the other; these qualities are two sides of the same coin. With them it was "root hog or die," and they rooted. Also, it was trade or perish, and they traded. Trade is possible only among those who are honest—who fulfill their promises—which means that they are self-responsible and free.

People from many lands came to find an explanation for the miracle of America, an outburst of creative energy never before witnessed. Alexis de Tocqueville found the right an-swer: "America is great because America is good. When America ceases to be good, America will cease to be great."

Our forefathers feared political tyranny. It never entered their heads to fear self-responsibility and its correlate, free-dom. People do not fear the righteousness from which they benefit.

Our early American ancestors feared political tyranny because they were physically close to it; it breathed down their necks. Under the circumstances, there was worse to fear than freedom. But, as each succeeding generation receded further from the experience of tyranny—possessing little if any understanding of the effects upon men of restraint and release—people came to be less and less fearful of authoritarianism. By 1974, there are comparatively few among us who fear political management.

As the fear of political tyranny disappears, the fear of freedom and self-responsibility mounts, until many may be found praying thus: "Oh, Great White Father, protect me from whoever would labor for less than I; from whoever would undersell me; from the lack of possessions which I think are my due. Give unto me my cravings." Responsibility for self has become nearly unthinkable.

There will be a return to freedom, regardless of present fears. Freedom is ordained in the Cosmic Order. Freedom will arise again and from either of two sources: (1) According to the historical pattern, it will arise from the ashes of dictocratic government, that is, after a people have been reduced to a shambles. Freedom is assured then, for it is the only alternative to extinction. But when? How long? This is the nonrational sequence for which there is no answer. (2) Our hope lies in an intellectual and moral awakening. Why should we not have a hand in shaping our destiny! Why must we be helpless pawns of a sequence void of human intelligence! For that intellectual and moral awakening, we need to realize that:

1. All dictocratic control of creative action must, of neces-

sity, be erroneous, for it destroys the innovative talent with which each of us is endowed by God.

2. Such dictocratic control is, by its nature, irresponsible. The dictocrats do not suffer the immediate penalty for their errors; we do!

3. We become irresponsible when we surrender self-responsibility or have it coercively taken from us. It is impossible to be responsible for anything that falls beyond one's own freedom of choice—and control!

4. Being one's own man is better than existing as a mere fraction of a collective. Self-responsibility is the joyous key to being human!

In the light of such understanding, Americans will no longer fear to be free. To love righteousness or intelligence or outstanding talent or virtue of any sort is to love freedom!

14

INEQUALITY ENSHRINED

*It is not true that equality is the law
of nature: nature has made nothing
equal.*
—MARQUIS DE VANVENARGUES

Books, speeches, expressed yearnings—past and present—
have much to say in favor of equality, and they promote a
demand for it. We are equal in the eyes of God, they say; we
are equal before the law; we are born equal, have equal
rights, are entitled to equal pay, on and on. While numerous
philosophers and statesmen have recognized how all-pervad-
ing inequality is, few have enshrined it, that is, portrayed inequality as a highly desirable state of affairs. Inequality exists, unfortunately! I have just had a change of mind:
inequality exists, *fortunately*!

In an earlier book I wrote:

> The authors of the Declaration took the rational step of
> seating the Creator as the single point of reference, thereby
> making all men precisely as *equal* before the civil law as all
> men are *equal* before the Creator.[1]

---

[1]See *To Free or Freeze* (Irvington-on-Hudson, N.Y.: Foundation for
Economic Education, Inc., 1972), p. 124.

We have here a semantic trap in which most of us—myself included—have become ensnared. Once we accept the idea that all men are equal before God, we are more than likely to think of equality as the major purpose of human effort and a condition to be sought, as nearly as possible, in all worldly relationships. This is a dangerous notion, completely at odds with reality.

As I now see it, men are no more equal before God than they are equal in this earthly life. Judas was not the equal of Peter! To contend otherwise is to condemn God as near-sighted. What this affirmation is intended to convey, really, is that all men are subject to the Universal Laws *indiscriminately; there are no favorites; there is a common across-the-board justice.* With this in mind, merely reflect on the distinction between common justice and equality. They are by no means synonymous.

Inequality prevails among men. One is a teetotaler, another an alcoholic. Joe is a genius at this, Bob at that. This man peers through a telescope to fathom the heavens; another through a microscope to probe the infinitesimal.

As F. A. Hayek concludes in *The Constitution of Liberty:*

From the fact that people are very different it follows that, if we treat them equally, the result must be inequality in their actual position, and that the only way to place them in an equal position would be to treat them differently. Equality before the law and material equality are therefore not only different but are in conflict with each other; and we can achieve either the one or the other, but not both at the same time.

The ideal civil law, like the laws of God or Natural Law, is unbiased as to who or what we are. But we are not equal in the "eyes" of the civil law any more than we are equal in the "eyes" of the Ten Commandments. These laws are blind; they have no eyes to see us. Civil laws, as the Universal Laws —if intelligently drawn—are indiscriminate; they confer no special privilege on anyone; they are but codes—blind to the thousand and one ways we rank ourselves—their hallmark being a common justice.

If we wish to say that these codes are equally as fair to you as to me, all well and good. This kind of wording, however, merely asserts that we are—one as much as another—beneficiaries of fairness and justice. By employing the right words, we avoid the notion of human equality and the mischievous deductions that grow from such a common, semantic error. I am agreeing with an observation by George Horne:

> Among the sources of those innumerable calamities which from age to age have overwhelmed mankind, may be reckoned as one of the principal, *the abuse of words.*

What about the popular claim that we are born equal? We are no more equal at birth than at death; no more equal in the fetus than in the grave. "Nature has made nothing equal," including all forms of nonlife or life, human or otherwise.[2]

We have equal rights! Valid? In a way, provided "rights" are properly defined and circumscribed. Any person, regardless of race, creed, color, or whatever, has as much right to life, livelihood, liberty as any other—provided his actions are peaceful, that is, noncoercive. Observe that when thus circumscribed, the equal rights concept makes no claim on any

---

[2]See *You Are Extraordinary* by Roger J. Williams (New York: Random House, 1967).

other person; it is, instead, *an appeal to reason, morality, justice*. It has no more muscle, no more teeth to it, than an aspiration. It is righteous and, for this reason, utterly harmless.

I stress "harmless" simply because most people put no such boundaries on "equal rights." Blind to the rational limitations of this concept, they are carried away with "equality" and demand equal pay, rights to a job, to "a decent standard of living," to a "fair" wage or price. They put quotas, embargoes, tariffs on goods, meaning that they think of themselves as having a right to your and my trade. It is impossible to list the instances in which people have slumped so far in their thinking that, today, mere wishes are thought of as rights.[3]

Take note of the fact that all of these demands for equality, beyond the rational boundary, make a claim on others. No longer harmless, they are harmful, destructive. They rob selected Peter to pay collective Paul—feathering the nests of some at the expense of others. Noncoercive? To the contrary, each and every one of these rests on raw coercion—the application of police force. Name an exception!

Sadly, the misunderstanding and misuse of the word "equality" accounts substantially for the leveling programs—egalitarianism—going on in the world today: communism, socialism, state welfarism, interventionism, and the like. Equality? I am for inequality!

The notion of equality is one of the mistaken features of our folklore, but so much lip service is given to it that the

---

[3]See "When Wishes Become Rights" in my book, *Deeper Than You Think* (Irvington-on-Hudson, N.Y.: Foundation for Economic Education, Inc., 1967), pp. 98-107.

thought of inequality as a desirable condition is, at first blush, shocking. How could any sane person favor inequality! Is it because he has no compassion, no thought for his fellow men? To the contrary, I would argue.

Man in his quest for perfection—for a growth in awareness, perception, consciousness—can make headway only to the extent that he perceives and abides by the Universal Laws. Conceded, our awareness of these Laws is infinitesimal; we know but very few of them. There is one, however, about which there can be no question: *inequality!* "Nature has made nothing equal."

No two atoms, molecules, snowflakes, planets, stars, galaxies are ever identical. No two persons are equal; indeed, no individual in any given moment of time is equal to himself in the previous moment. Imagine—a million new red blood cells every second! All is radiant energy, in one form or another; all is in motion from imperceptible slowness to the speed of light. Is this as it should be? My answer is "yes," for this is the way it is—like it or not. I like it!

A further demonstration that this thesis is a "switch" for me: In *Who's Listening?* I had a chapter entitled "How To Be Like Socrates." One friend wrote, "I don't want to be like Socrates." I got a chuckle, but not the point—until later.

Suppose—I thought to myself—everyone *were* like Socrates. We would all be on the street asking each other a series of easily answered questions that inevitably lead the answerer to a logical conclusion foreseen by the questioner. Everybody would be slovenly, ugly, and wise. No one would be raising food, or building homes, or making planes, stoves, pots, pans. Indeed, were all like Socrates, there would not be a person on this earth.

Likeness? Equality? Let us be done with this careless phrasing—this abuse of words—and the destructive thoughts to which it leads!

"Free and equal" is an oft-heard expression, suggesting that freedom and equality are as inseparable as Siamese twins. Actually, they are mutually antagonistic. The equality idea—equal pay and so on—rests on the antithesis of freedom: raw coercion. It is just as impossible to be free when equality is politically manipulated as it is impossible to be equal.

Free and unequal—freedom and inequality—are what go hand in hand. The essence of individuality is uniqueness: inequality in skills, talents, knowledge, aspirations. This is merely an acknowledgment of a Universal Law. Obviously, we must be free to produce, to exchange, to travel or we perish as surely as if all were like you or me or Socrates.

We come, finally, to the economic case for inequality. Not our likenesses, but our differences, give rise to the division of labor and the complex market processes of production and trade. We have already mentioned, and can see all about us, that in a given field of activity one person is more skilled— more productive—than another. So, it is to our advantage to specialize and to trade with other specialists.

This is not to say that each of us must be equally skilled as a specialist in order for him to gain the advantages of trade. The more skilled one becomes at his speciality, the greater his incentive to hire or trade with others to carry out certain tasks for him, even though he can cook meals or scrub floors better than can the person he hires for such tasks. It is to his comparative advantage to concentrate his efforts on the single skill for which consumers offer him the greatest reward. By thus serving others—and becoming ever more skilled and outstanding (unequal) in the process—he best serves his own interest.

A moment's reflection reveals that this comparative advantage in trading, which rewards the most renowned specialist, also rewards in similar fashion every other party to such trade, down to the very least-skilled participant in the market. This is not to say that their gains would be equal; only that each gains from the trade more goods and services than otherwise would have been his. And what is true here of trade between individuals in a given nation is also true of international trade. However wealthy or poor and skilled or unskilled the respective traders, each finds a comparative advantage in trading—if it is voluntary.

Not only does this blessing of inequality flow from the mental or physical skills of traders; it also pertains to the capital, the tools of the trade, the savings and investments by individuals. The specialist who saves and develops tools becomes ever more specialized and efficient. And it is to the advantage of every participant in the market to encourage the saver and investor by respecting and protecting his property —even though the result is greater inequality of wealth than before. Otherwise, there soon would be no incentive for anyone to save or invest in the tools of production, the facilities of trade.

So, if a people would avoid falling to a low level of sameness and bare subsistence, the procedure is to cultivate and accentuate their differences in skills and in private ownership and use of property—these being the requisites for a flourishing and beneficial trade. And let us bear in mind that exchange (other than primitive barter) depends on an honest, trustworthy, circulating medium; this is an absolute—money of integrity. Freedom in monetary matters means no political manipulation of our medium of exchange.

That, in brief, is the economic case for inequality.[4] Sadly, the misunderstanding and misapplication of the concept of "equality" affords a major explanation for the leveling programs—egalitarianism—going on in the world today: communism, socialism, state welfarism, interventionism, and the like. So, I take my stand for inequality.

Let us then enshrine inequality by acknowledging and embracing this fact of Nature—inequality—and, also, its working handmaiden: human freedom. Allow no interference with creative activities, which is to say, permit anyone to do anything he chooses so long as it is peaceful. A fair field and no favor!

---

[4]A more detailed treatment of these arguments may be found in pages 836-847 of *Human Action* by Ludwig von Mises.

15

THE REVEALING SELF

Example is the school of mankind;
they will learn at no other.
— EDMUND BURKE

It took Spinoza, a philosopher of three centuries ago, to awaken me to the startling fact that all of my writings, lectures, expressions of likes and dislikes, tell far more about me than they do about the subjects to which I address myself. It was a shock to realize that I reveal the kind of person I am more than I convey the ideas I intend! And you, whatever your rank or status, are rarely an exception to this rule.

The awakening line was this: "Paul's idea of Peter tells us more about Paul than about Peter." Indeed, plausible! But this was the clincher: "The prophets' ideas about God tell us more about the prophets than about God."[1] Emerson echoed this idea when he remarked: "What you are speaks so loud I cannot hear what you say!"

---

[1] See *The Philosophy of Spinoza* by Joseph Ratner (New York: The Modern Library, Inc., 1927), pp. xiv-xlvi.

Two commentaries are warranted: (1) a briefing of Spinoza's philosophy that we may understand what led him to this conclusion and (2) the valuable instruction to be deduced that we may embrace and follow it. Conceded, I am including Spinoza as one of the rare exceptions to the rule being explored.

Goethe, one of the brilliant minds of our time, acknowledged that Spinoza was the only philosopher with whom he had no disagreement.[2] My favorite Goethe quotation, which I have twice cited already, is pure Spinoza:

> Nature understands no jesting; she is always true, always serious, always severe; she is always right, and the errors and faults are always those of man. The man incapable of appreciating her she despises, and only to the apt, the pure, and the true, does she resign herself and reveal her secrets.

Spinoza used the terms God and Nature interchangeably. He rejected the common idea of an anthropomorphic deity, viewing God, rather, as the immutable universal laws which man is powerless to alter. "Nothing finite is self-sufficient, only the infinite can be truly substantial and the separate things of existence and life are but aspects of infinite divinity. . . . In order to fulfill one's destiny it is necessary to seek understanding of the workings of the universe, to accommodate one's self as best one can to the infinite plan, and to

---

[2]Boldly, I have several disagreements with Spinoza, none more pronounced than this: "Far from it being necessary to tell the masses only the truth Spinoza believed, as did Plato before him, that it may even be necessary in order to rule the masses successfully in the ways of wisdom and virtue to deceive them to a greater or lesser extent. Such deception is, as a political expediency, morally justified, for the rulers would be lying in the interests of virtue and truth." (Ratner, p. xlvi) This argues that the end justifies the means. Is this excusable on the grounds that the free society was, in Spinoza's time, an unborn concept? Emphatically not!

participate in it. [It is] *realizing the self as part of the unlimited.*"[3] (Italics added)

True, Spinoza is one of those rare exceptions to the rule in
question. Nonetheless, his recorded insights tell far more
about him than they tell about the eternal verities he attempted to explain.

Return to the prophets. What, for instance, did they with
their finite minds know of infinite divinity—God or Nature?
True, they experienced many enlightenments but, relative to
the infinite unknown, their glimmerings were no more than
wee candles. The point to note is this: they told us a great
deal more about themselves and their thinking than about
God. Similarly, what does any Paul know of any Peter? Substantially nothing! Indeed, no one—Paul and Peter included—
gains more than a smattering of his own makeup and being.
Paul, in his assessment of Peter, reveals far more about Paul
than about Peter!

In a word, one's messages are viewed not so much for their
subject matter, as is commonly thought, but far more for what
they reveal of the writer or speaker. He is being looked at,
sized up, assessed. The reader or listener, even though he
may not realize it, is trying to discover what kind of a person
Paul was, you are, I am.

What am I to make of this discovery? Should it dampen
or enliven my spirit and efforts? Frankly, I have seldom come
upon a more encouraging guideline. Why this exuberance?
My answer: In writing this, for instance, it is I, far more than
my explanations, that will be revealed. Is this not an incentive
to put the best foot forward, to present openly and honestly

---

[3]See *The Columbia Encyclopedia,* Second Edition, p. 1863.

one's highest thoughts? Indeed, an incentive *par excellence!*

Have a look at this from the usual and negative angle. Reflect on the countless people who are commenting angrily on "the mess we are in," the name callers, those who are throwing in the sponge, giving up the ghost. Actually, they reveal only themselves; they do nothing to enlighten us about our personal and societal troubles. Carefully examine your own assessments in the light of Spinoza's observation and note how correct it is.

Anyone who grasps this simple point cannot help but turn himself toward man's most important role: examplarity, that is, to do all within his power to strive for the best he can possibly attain. Imagine a citizenry so oriented! Were enough of us suddenly to thus aim our thoughts, words, actions we could, possibly, expect to turn the world around in eighty days! It is, as Spinoza asserts, "realizing the self as part of the unlimited."

Edmund Burke phrased a great truth: "Example is the school of mankind; they will learn at no other." Exemplarity in its purest form is contagious, for all gains in the higher realms of thought are caught, not taught.

How describe those rare occasions when you or I go beyond sizing up another, taking his measure, so to speak? At what point does exemplarity become contagious? In my own case, it is when someone's attainment reaches unusually attractive heights still within my sights. It is when another is deemed to be much above my level, whose thoughts I can look up to. This is when I go beyond assessing his person and try instead to partake of his enlightenment. It is a fair wager that this holds true for you also. Thank you, Baruch de Spinoza, for a valuable lesson!

16

RAILING AGAINST FOLLY

*However, not a word more upon
this wretched subject, lest I become unwise in railing against
folly.*

—GOETHE

Goethe's observation about railing against folly came during
the 83rd and last year of his life. Another translation reads,
". . . lest I fall into unreason while fighting the unreasonable."[1] Translated either way, this raises some important
questions—as germaine to our time as to Goethe's.

Does railing against folly, in fact, cause one to become unwise, to fall into unreason? If one decides never to rail against
folly, how then is a concerned person to treat the "wretched"
subjects heard on every hand? Must one infer that these
should be ignored? Or, having made such a decision, does
there remain a way of coping with follies? Were enough of us
to know the correct answers to these questions and were we

---

[1]Here is the way it reads in the original German: Doch kein Wort mehr
über diesen schlechten Gegenstand, damit ich nicht unvernünftig werde, in-
dem ich das Unvernünftige bekämpfe.

to put the knowledge into practice, I am convinced that the present wayward trend would be reversed. My aim here is to search for the right answers.

Goethe's fear, I believe, is well founded; we do fall into unreason if we choose to fight it out at the folly levels. If someone claims that the moon is made of green cheese and I elect to debate him at his level, my rebuttals will smack as much of green-cheese nonsense as his silly assertion. When one goes to the gutter to set the world straight he will, sooner or later, become a guttersnipe himself. He nails his thinking down to unreason.

It is impossible to list the thousand and one follies which daily assail us. They range all the way from claims by celebrated "economists" that politicians can run our lives better than we can, to feathering one's own nest at the expense of others, to wage and price controls.

Let me concede, before going further, that these numerous follies are not, by and large, consciously malicious. Most of them are inspired by good intentions. What then accounts for the originators getting so far off the track? No one knows all the answers. However, there is one reason which deserves reflection—a seeming confusion between private businessmanship and governmental statesmanship, these being two distinctly different realms.

What is one of the sound procedures for an honest soup maker, for instance? It is to contrive a concoction that will satisfy palates—the more the better. His own taste for soup is not the guideline; rather, it is the taste of soup consumers. It is they, not he, whose tastes direct the kinds of soup he produces.

As to the governmental realm, we must concede that the

quality of officeholders is but an echoing of voter thinking. If it be low, politicians will occupy the seats of political power; if high, statesmen will preside.

When the thinking of voters is low, they will elect those who will cater to their something-for-nothing whims—political soup makers—men who promise to use their coercive power to gratify tastes, however degenerate they may be. But blame not the politician for aping the soup makers; it is the voters, not he, whose tastes direct the plundering and sharing operations. This, I believe, is one of the reasons why the originators of folly get so far off the track.

If, on the other hand, the thinking of voters were high grade, those elected to office would be statesmen, men who would stand ramrod straight for what they personally believed to be right and just—no special favor—or flavor—to anyone! If there were less demand for folly, there would be fewer producers of it.

I am contending that the politicians who respond to the folly market are more or less blind to their mischief. They use the highly approved soup maker's formula for success. Why should there be a different tactic for staying in office than for staying in business! In a word, the ways of material affluence have shut their eyes to moral perfection. To close our own eyes, which is what we do when railing against their follies— name calling, confrontations—adds nothing to their enlightenment while it stifles our own. It is said that when the blind try to lead the blind, both fall into the ditch. Did you ever see a person brighten up when called "Stupid"? Never, any more than the name caller brightened up! Railing is blinding to the railed at and to the railer.

Railing against nonsense is no answer; it is self-defeating.

What then about these "wretched" subjects? Must we shut our eyes to them? Ignore these follies as if nonexistent? Have we who wish to avoid becoming unwise or unreasonable relegated ourselves to the do-nothing, helpless scrap heap? To the contrary! By closing the door to the wrong way, the one that leads only to darkness, the door to the right way opens to our view, the one that leads to light—our own enlightenment.

Instead of railing against follies, rally in search of truth! What does this type of action suggest? Rather than uselessly berating this and that folly, think through and learn how to explain what should replace it. For instance:

- If more people understood the efficacy of private ownership and freedom in transactions, wage and price controls would get no more hearing than "the earth is flat."
- If the truth were recognized that no living person can coercively control the creative life of another beneficially, the whole dictocratic structure would tumble into a shambles.
- If it were more generally believed that the way out of poverty is not "from each according to ability, to each according to need," but, rather, to each according to production, the feathering of the nests of some at the expense of others would be at an end.
- If virtues and talents—morality—were riding high, that is, if each were accurately reflecting what his highest conscience dictates as righteous, statesmen would replace politicians.

One might go on and on with these examples, but the point is clear. We need only bear in mind that folly gives way to truth precisely as darkness recedes when light increases.

Yes, follies do indeed merit our attention. They suggest the areas in need of enlightenment, subjects on which our creative attention should be focused.

It is light that brings forth the eye. Seek enlightenment! Whose eyes will open? One's own, for certain! And, if the light be bright enough, some others will also see. Perhaps even a politician or two, but that does not matter. If others see, the folly collaborators will be unseated; no longer will they occupy positions of power. It is *what* is seen, not *who* sees.

So, forget railing against folly and, instead, accent what's right. This is the answer which, if practiced, will keep you and me from falling into unreason, from becoming unwise. Further, it will reverse the present waywardness.

17

TIME-LAPSE THINKING

Economics ... is the science of trac-
ing the effects of some proposed or
existing policy not only on some
special *interest* in the short run, *but*
on the general *interest* in the long
run.[1]

— **HENRY HAZLITT**

Most politico-economic policies in our time are in response to
the demands of this or that special interest or pressure group,
while the general interest is ignored. Further, the long-run effect is overlooked in order that short-run "gains" may be
achieved. This is the road to disaster, and no turnabout is
possible short of a greater reliance on time-lapse thinking. Let
Walt Disney's demonstration explain what I mean by time-
lapse thinking.

Disney planted a rose seedling and made a motion picture
of its growth, flicking a single frame every day or so until the
plant was mature and the rose had bloomed. When he showed
this film on a screen at sixteen frames per second, we then

---

[1]See *Economics in One Lesson* (N.Y.: Manor Books), p. 135.

witnessed the whole beautiful phenomenon—the unfolding of a rosebud—in a minute or two. Disney's time-lapse photography enabled us to experience an improvement in frequency perception; that is, the viewers were able to see the long-run effects of short-run causes. This is why I suggest the urgency of some time-lapse thinking.

While time-lapse photography and time-lapse thinking are similar in that each collapses time, there is an important difference. The former reduces the time between causes and effects that have already taken place; the latter requires that time be collapsed as related to future effects of present causes. True, no person has a crystal ball, nor could he read it if he had one. Yet, I believe there is a way of foreseeing what effects certain actions will have.

Carry this belief a step further. The easiest and perhaps the only way to be certain that a short-run action is a gain or loss is to discover what its long-run effects will be. Why? *There is no such thing as a short-run gain that is not also a long-run gain, and vice versa.* As Emerson wrote, "The end pre-exists in the means." It is axiomatic that constructive service of the individual's purposes or of the general interest can never emerge from destructive means. Thus, collapse time, resort to time-lapse thinking, to evaluate day-to-day actions.

To illustrate: Is thievery a short-run gain for the thief? Most thieves think it is or they would not steal. Having a stunted perception, they fail to realize that the loss in life-values far exceeds the gain in loot. Were the thief capable of time-lapse thinking, he would clearly see that a population of thieves would perish. The long-run effect would be disastrous; therefore, the short-run action—the means—is disastrous and evil.

Direct theft is practiced by comparatively few of the total population. Most people find it unnecessary to do time-lapse thinking to put thievery in its proper place. However, millions of these same people not only condone but participate in legal plunder, that is, they urge government to do the looting for them. They see nothing wrong with this; indeed, they regard the loot as a gain. Perhaps the only way for them to set their thinking straight is a resort to time-lapse thinking.

In a nutshell, let these millions project their practices into the future—everyone doing what the few are now doing, that is, everyone being paid for not working. Clearly, were there no work there would be no loot to take, nothing to plunder. As with thievery, all would perish. By the simple device of collapsing time, the future effect of their present actions would become obvious. Thus, living off others is not even a short-run gain. A few paltry dollars at the price of surrendering responsibility for self—the very essence of being—amounts to an enormous net loss.

Many farmers get paid for not farming and regard the payments as gains. Apply this political nostrum to all productive activity, not only getting paid for not farming but getting paid for not generating electricity, not drilling for and refining oil, not making clothes and autos, and so on. Project such practices into the future and observe the self-evident consequences. Time-lapse thinking will reveal the fallacy; it will serve as an eye-opener, a needed shock treatment. All losses *now!*

Reflect on the businessmen who seek political protection against competition, domestic as well as foreign. Assume the universality of this craving for short-run "gains" and then assess the future. What would be the economic picture?

What would it look like? Ancient feudalism or medieval mercantilism or modern communism!

No need for more illustrations; a thousand and one could be cited. Time-lapse thinking not only is invaluable in deciding on sound economic policy but can be used to arrive at the correctness of present actions in all fields—education, religion, politics, or whatever.

From such thinking stems this helpful conclusion: fret not for the morrow, only for today. Why? Because the morrow is a life-style edifice structured from today's actions. Wrote Addison: "This is the world of seeds, of causes, and of tendencies; the other is the world of harvests and results and of perfected and eternal consequences." Thus, if today's actions are as right as one can make them, then the morrow is as good as it can be.

My gratitude to Henry Hazlitt for his philosophy, and to Walt Disney for his technology. I have merely strung their pearls of wisdom on a single thread.

18

BUY AMERICAN

He that hath a trade hath an estate;
and he that hath a calling hath a
place of profit and honor. A plow-
man on his legs is higher than a
gentleman on his knees.

—**FRANKLIN**

The admonition to "Buy American" has two diametrically opposed meanings. The first is its popular and mischievous meaning—shun goods produced in foreign countries. The second, and loftier meaning embodied in these words, is rarely mentioned or thought of—shun principles and practices alien to the American dream of limited government and personal freedom.

Producers who plead with consumers to "Buy American" are appealing to blind patriotism. Buy my product because it is made here; heed not its price or quality. This is sheer chauvinism. Suppose I were to urge your acceptance of my ideas, rather than those of Marx or Machiavelli, merely because of our differing nationalities. The absurdity of such an appeal is obvious: neither goods nor ideas are properly judged in this fashion; geographical origin has nothing to do with the matter.

While the plea, "Buy American," is less frequently heard in these words than formerly, the notion persists, however subtle and varied its phrasing. All obstacles to competition, be they foreign or domestic, are but variants of this theme. For instance, barriers exist by the thousands between states and even cities. A few examples will suffice to make my point.

Try to buy Florida oranges and grapefruit in California!

I recall when General Manager of the Los Angeles Chamber of Commerce the trouble we had in defeating a resolution that would impose a restriction on the entry of Kansas beef. After all, there is quite a cattle industry in Southern California!

How many times have we heard the local chamber of commerce plea: "Buy at home; protect our merchants and industries." Here we have the "Buy American" nonsense brought from the international to the Main Street level.

Don't get caught bringing cigarettes into New York which you bought in New Jersey, or the booze you purchased in Illinois into Indiana. A tariff? No! But it amounts to the same thing: a "fair trade" law in one and not the other or higher state taxes in one than the other. Goods will tend to move illegally from the lower priced to the higher area—via black marketeers!

Frankly, we should not assess this trend as nation, state, or city control. Call it by its right name: *People control*! What's the difference between the plea, "Buy American," and the demand from union bosses that all union members—and everyone else—buy only goods produced under union label?

All wage and price controls, whether rent control in New York City, freezes by the Federal government, minimum wage laws, or above-market wages and below-market hours coercively exacted by labor unions, are people control. These rigidities are not to be distinguished from the "Buy American" or "Buy at home" notion. When prices, for instance, are fixed below the market, producers are threatened with loss or bankruptcy. The political remedy? Impose tariffs, quotas, embargoes against foreign competition in order to relieve domestic producers. In a word, force consumers to "Buy American!"

Enough of this mischievous notion. Let us try instead to appreciate and "buy" the American ideal of freedom.

In what respect was the American idea unique? Wrote Daniel Webster:

[America] holds out an example a thousand times more encouraging than ever was presented before to those nine-tenths of the human race who are born without hereditary fortune or hereditary rank.

Ralph Waldo Emerson had this to say:

America is another name for opportunity. Our whole history appears like a last effort of divine Providence in behalf of the human race.

While numerous individuals might be singled out, Benjamin Franklin qualifies as well as anyone as an exemplar of the unique political structure known as America. "As American as apple pie."[1] My explanation later.

As to the best in political economy, consider the Constitution of the United States. Regardless of its several flaws, no other nation's charter has equalled it in an economic sense.

---

[1]A biography of Franklin by John Tottle was entitled *Benjamin Franklin: The First Great American.*

In what respect is this distinctively American? Here is the answer:

> No state shall without the consent of the Congress, lay any imposts on imports and exports. . . .

In a nutshell, no tariffs, quotas, embargoes between the several states. While the British Empire in its heyday had a larger free trade area when measured in square miles, the world has never known a free trade area as large as the U.S.A. when measured in value of goods and services produced and exchanged. Never perfectly free, but the nearest approximation to freedom!

Take Western Europe with all of its contiguous nations, each country walled off from the others by many trade barriers, custom houses, border guards. Then reflect on the U.S.A. which has more states than Europe has nations. Unless watching the map or the road signs, rarely can one tell when crossing from one state to another. Compare the wealthiest European nation with the least wealthy state in our Union and the latter has it by a mile. Why? The free market here more than there!

One of the flaws in early America was a moderate tariff. There were two excuses: (1) revenue and (2) to protect our "infant industries" against the competition of European giants. Here are three questions and their answers:

1. What nation in all the world and in all history has had the most infant industrial starts? The U.S.A.
2. In what nation has there been the greatest number of infant industries growing into giants? In the U.S.A.
3. In what nation has this little-to-bigness development faced the greatest competition? In the U.S.A. where

there have been and are now more industrial giants than have ever existed elsewhere.

In reality, it is competition which protects "infant industries"; it protects them from stagnation and persuades them to grow.

In the absence of competition and freedom of transactions, producers stagnate. It is only when others are doing better that one attempts to overcome, to gain strength. Competition, combined with free exchange, makes strong giants out of weak infants; this is the password to economic opportunity and well-being—an American idea well worth buying.

Regardless of all the noisy arguments to the contrary, everyone known to me favors both competition and free trade. Name one who does not favor competition among those from whom he buys. Logically, then, how can one favor competition among millions of others and be against it for himself! This is irrationality, not disagreement.

Precisely the same can be said for free trade—domestic or foreign. Name one who would not welcome an order for his products from another country or county. Everyone favors exports. Imports? Favoring exports and objecting to imports is the same as favoring selling and objecting to being paid. This is an absurdity, not disagreement.

To conclude this examination of the Americanism worth buying, I return to Franklin whom I consider the first great American economist.

Prior to the more or less simultaneous discoveries by the Austrian, Menger, the Englishman, Jevons, and the Swiss, Walras—around 1870—nearly everyone, economists included, agreed with the Frenchman, Montaigne, that one man's gain had to be someone else's loss.

The reason for this economic blindness was a failure to understand value. The false idea was that the value of a good was the cost of its production or, as it is called, the labor theory of value. Menger, Jevons, and Walras, by observing how people behave when free, reputedly discovered the subjective theory of value, perhaps the most important discovery in economic history. It was simply this: the value of any good or service is whatever anyone will offer in willing exchange. Rather than one gaining and another losing, each gains, according to his own subjective judgment. Otherwise, there would be no swap.

And now I learn of Franklin's prescience. "The First Great American," a century earlier than Menger, made this observation:

> In transactions of trade it is not to be supposed that, as in gaming, what one party gains the other must necessarily lose. The gain to each may be equal. If A. has more corn than he can consume, but wants cattle; and B. has more cattle, but wants corn; exchange is gain to each; thereby the *common stock of comforts in life is increased*. (Italics added)

How much Franklin's insight—ahead of his time—had to do with early America cannot be determined; doubtless, it was substantial. For our forefathers freely traded; they were as anxious to buy as to sell. What perturbed them greatly was a tax on tea.

Combining the Constitution's establishment of free trade among the states and Franklin's correct theory of value, what then is meant by "Buy American" in its proper sense?

Let willing exchange prevail among all people, locally and

worldwide. Let each buyer or seller be guided by his own scale of values. Sell the American way and buy the American way—not as presently practiced, but as once prevailed and ought to be reinstituted. Keep ours the land of opportunity for everyone. "A plowman on his legs is higher than a gentleman on his knees."

19

REVERENCE, THAT ANGEL OF THE WORLD

Always and in everything let there be reverence.

—CONFUCIUS

Moral philosophy is the study of right and wrong. Economics is a branch thereof: the study of right and wrong as the results bear upon the overcoming of scarcity. The tendency among most "economists" and many free market devotees is to concentrate on the branch, economics, while ignoring the tree, morality. Indeed, ever so many deem it quixotic to do otherwise; to bring morality into the problem of scarcity is to climb aboard "cloud 9"; it is to go into reverie or daydreams. Such aspersions are utter folly, for if the tree be rotten the branch is dead!

To make my point, assume every American to be as knowledgeable in economics as the renowned Ludwig von Mises, but utterly devoid of moral scruples. The economic knowledge would be misused. The aim of maximizing comfort while minimizing effort would lead to political means for the enriching of some at the expense of others. This, in turn, would diminish productivity and introduce scarcity. Scarcity and immorality,

104

in fact, go hand in hand precisely as do scarcity and thievery. Try to imagine a society of thieves! In vain; parasites die in the absence of a host. We are forced to conclude that scarcity is best overcome when all are hosts—producers—and none are thieves.

Thievery is on the rampage the world over. While overwhelmingly in the form of legalized plunder, it is as parasitical as the personal holdup variety. Unless checked, it must eventually destroy the hosts.

Stealing, evil as it is, falls short of killing when it comes to man's inhumanity to man. This, also, is on the rampage and is condoned, if not directly participated in, by millions of citizens in the wars of our age. By far the vast majority of those who approve of the mass slaughter going on in the world today would not personally kill a man, woman, or child. They would prefer their own death to such an offense. Yet, collectivize the action, let it bear the label of government, and all sense of personal guilt vanishes. The feeling is nearly unanimous, "I'm not responsible!" Find even one who thinks of himself as a killer! In consequence of such moral blindness and sloppy thinking tens of thousands have gone to their reward. In any event, let no one, economist or whoever, suggest that ours is not, first and foremost, a moral problem.

It is this line of thought which emphasizes—to me, at least—that sound economic practices are out of the question except as they stem from and are an outgrowth of moral rectitude. The abundant life can no more emerge from immoral behavior than a Statue of Liberty can be built on quicksand. Thus, heed not the counselor who prescribes recipes for more goods and services and omits the essential ingredient: morality! The staff of life—bread—is not made from water alone.

Irreverence seems to be the mood of our time; it is noted all about us. Not only is there a general irreverence for the fruits of another's labor—legal plunder—but there is an appalling irreverence for human life. Indeed, there is little if any difference between taking the subsistence of life and taking life itself. Who cares whether he is starved or stabbed to death!

The cure for irreverence, and the only one, is reverence—a reverence for life, all life. One wonders how that man, Shakespeare, referred to this virtue as "That angel of the world"—a flash of enlightenment come upon nearly four centuries ago, an insight that is rarely thought of in our time, let alone mentioned![1]

It has been my conviction for several years that those of us who favor the freedom philosophy and the superior way of life it makes possible, have been derelict in our explanations; we have been overlooking numerous obscure underpinnings of the philosophy and, in consequence, have failed miserably to make our own case. Reverence for life is indeed an "angel"; it is a virtue to which we must wed ourselves or pay the exorbitant price of irreverence, that is, pay with our lives, no less!

I am the first to admit that a reverence for life—all life, be it plant or animal—is difficult to come by; the awakening must stem from an experience not common to life as we live it today.

Until 17 years ago I did not differ from the mill run of peo-

---

[1]An outstanding exception is Albert Schweitzer, a man of many talents. See the chapter, "The Ethic of Reverence for Life," in *Albert Schweitzer: The Man and His Mind* by George Seaver (New York: Harper & Brothers, 1947).

ple so far as a reverence for *all* life is concerned. To use a Davy Crockett term, it took a "sockdolager" to bring me to myself. I share this not with the expectation that my experience will suffice for anyone else but merely to explain my own awakening. The "sockdolager," an entry in my journal, is entitled, *LE DERNIER TESTAMENT D'UN CANARD.* It reads thus:

The following explanation is pasted on the back of this painting in case any of LER's progeny ever have a curiosity as to what inspired this sad scene. Why is the title in French? The duck's expression had to be deduced by grandpappy just as grandpappy always had to guess what a Frenchman was saying.

"It was a Sunday, October 28, 1956. Len, Jr., and I were in the blinds at 5:30 A.M. at his duck club near Dos Palos, California. There was neither cloud nor breeze. On Wednesday we had had our two limits in an hour—all sprig. On Saturday it had taken us four hours to obtain twenty birds. This Sunday, however, held little promise, for only now and then would a bird come within gunshot.

"I was not doing well at all. Of a sudden, after nearly three hours of relative inactivity, a flock of teal flew by, a little too far away, but possible. My single shot brought down three birds, one dead and two injured—luck like a hole-in-one. Len had no trouble retrieving the crippled and dead birds as I went in search of the other. Eventually, I found this male teal, snuggled against a tuft of water grass, the saddest sight I have ever seen. One tiny pellet from the gunshot had penetrated his left eye. Three drops of blood stained his pretty feathers. His head was turned toward me as I approached, his whole demeanor being not of anger, but, as it seemed to me, of quiet reproach for taking the life of an innocent little fellow—just for fun!

"This picture remained vividly in my memory. On November 20th I phoned Lloyd Sanford, a wildlife artist of the New York Zoological Society, and described the scene to him. The next day his pencil sketch was on my desk. Sanford had caught my impression perfectly.

"This, then is the last testament of a dying duck, stored in my subconscious for nearly a month, communicated electrically to a sympathetic artist, and committed to an oil painting. The painting may never have an appropriate title, but the theme is clear: The teal doesn't appear to argue that man shouldn't kill ducks any more than ducks shouldn't kill fish. He seems only to convey a profound sorrow that an individual with my moral and spiritual pretensions should take the life of such as he while having the effrontery to call it sportsmanship."

Once "that angel of the world," as Shakespeare referred to reverence, insinuates itself into one's consciousness, it extends even to insect and plant life. The great Albert Schweitzer wouldn't chop down a tree to make way for a hospital; rather, he would transplant it. He was once observed flat on his belly scooping ants from a pile hole into which an ant hill had fallen. Is this carrying reverence for life too far? If so, then I am also an extremist. I have, for instance, taken hornets and wasps from the house on a piece of paper, freeing them to their outdoor kingdom. Never kill anything for the fun of it is the moral lesson that little teal taught me.[2]

---

[2]Aldous Huxley carries the matter one stage further. In conversation with a colleague of mine he remarked, "One hears it said that you shouldn't treat people as things. You shouldn't even treat things as things!"

Why dwell on these minutiae? Simply because reverence has its inception—birth—at these lower levels of life. Ingrained at this level, it extends as a moral compulsion into human relationships. He who would not kill a tree or bee for sport will never steal for aggrandizement or otherwise bring avoidable suffering to his fellow man. "Great oaks from little acorns grow"; great men from tiny ova flow; and precisely the same with reverence for life!

While pondering this subject, I came upon an article, "The Vanishing Kangaroo," an account of a sickening irreverence for life.[3]

> To see a kangaroo in bounding flight is to see nature at its best. To see a big Red chopped down by bullets while loping at 35 miles per hour is to see man at his worst.

And then this commentary:

> The willingness to save these gentle, amiable, almost defenseless creatures is important not only in keeping the kangaroos alive, but also *in keeping human.* (Italics added)

"In keeping human!" Should that not be modified to read, "On becoming human"? Were men to behave no more abominably toward each other than do animals and plants within their species, humans would at least be humane. Remember, a wolf never kills a wolf![4]

What is the popular way to correct this widespread irrever-

---

[3]See "The Vanishing Kangaroo" in *The American Way,* May 1973, by Derryn Hinch, Editor and Manager, *The Sydney Morning Herald,* Sydney, Australia.

[4]See "Morals and Weapons," the final chapter in *King Solomon's Ring* by Konrad Z. Lorenz, who, according to Julian Huxley, is "one of the outstanding naturalists of our times." In paperback (New York, N.Y.: Thomas Y. Crowell Co., 1961).

ence for life? Millions of people deplore what is happening to the kangaroos in Australia, to the wolves in Canada, to wild life all over the globe, and they want to do something. The prescription? Run to government! Pass a law! Reverence, the sole remedy for irreverence, can never be achieved in this manner. Reverence, "that angel of the world," is a spiritual achievement born, if at all, in the souls of discrete individuals. Reverence for life can no more be forced into existence by a constabulary—laws, edicts—than can the love of one for another. It is always a personal acquisition, never an imposition.

Admittedly, this subject is as "touchy" as it is delicate which is one reason why so few individuals with my point of view ever "stick their necks out." Why "touchy"? Most people have habits, a way of life as related to all life, so settled and ingrained that they never question whether their positions are right or wrong.

My next point may seem like a concession to irreverence but, really, it is not. Schweitzer concedes, and I agree, that all life lives on life. There is no exception. Vegetarians live on plant life. Thus, every form of life—man, animal, or plant—lives by consuming the living. Otherwise, there would be no life on this earth. From this fact, it follows that living off life cannot be classified as irreverence; this would be a contradiction for, if abandoned, there would be no one to show any reverence for anything.

What then is meant by a reverence for life? When may life be taken—plant or animal—other than to live? My answer: when it aggresses, invades, threatens to take over. Chop down weeds when they invade the garden, or do away with vermin or other pests when pestering. In a word, show reverence for animal and plant life except in instances of intrusion. Employ only defensive force!

It is my contention that if one had this degree and measure of reverence for all plant and animal life, he would quite naturally extend a similar reverence to all human life. This is to say that one would use only defensive, never aggressive, force. In this case, one would not take human life nor break the Commandment, "Thou shalt not kill." Let me explain.

If another aggresses—comes at me with a dagger, for instance—and is killed as I act in my own defense, it is he, not I, who is responsible for his demise. He initiated the action with its unfortunate result; he committed suicide!

That one should revere the Creator is readily conceded— at least by all truly religious people. Not all such people, however, have taken the logical step of extending reverence to all life—His creation.

It took a green wing teal, a form of life midway between plant and man, to improve my reverence for plant, animal, and man. Imagine my gratitude to that angel of reverence— in my case a bird!

20

SISYPHUS

*Let's make sisyphism a part of our
mythology instead of our national
policy.*

Sisyphus in Greek mythology was condemned, as a punishment for his wickedness in this life, to roll a stone from the bottom to the top of a hill. Whenever the stone reached the top it rolled down again. Thus, his task was never-ending.

The wickedness of Sisyphus was not a case of politico-economic intrigue. But Frederic Bastiat, the eminent French economist, philosopher, and statesman of well over a century ago, dubbed all people *sisyphists* who, by restrictive measures, tend to make the tasks of life unending.

Let us peek into the nature and extent of present-day *sisyphists* if only to create a desire among ourselves to reread some of the works of the great Bastiat and again to profit by his clarity of thought and simplicity of expression.[1] His

---

[1]See especially *The Law, Economic Sophisms, Economic Harmonies* and *Selected Essays on Political Economy* by Frederic Bastiat (Irvington-on-Hudson, N.Y.: The Foundation for Economic Education, Inc.).

fascinating parables could hardly have been more appropriate in his time than in ours.

The progress of human beings from a state of general impoverishment toward one of relative abundance is impeded by a series of *obstacles*. People who really serve society contribute to the overcoming of these obstacles, thereby creating abundance. Is it not precisely this kind of service whereby we may judge whether a business or a labor union or a government policy or official is social or antisocial?

People who perpetuate obstacles in order to maintain conditions of scarcity in their own line of production, thus keeping their efforts profitable at the expense of others, and who make the task of achieving abundance an endless one are, in Bastiat's estimation, *sisyphists*.

"There isn't work enough in our line for all you fellows wanting in. Keep out! By closed shops, closed unions, and closed associations we can create prosperity for ourselves and make our tasks here unending." Selfish *sisyphists*!

"Slow down on this job, fellows, and take more vacations, so our work will last longer." Lazy *sisyphists*!

"Competition is ruining our business. Let's put a stop to it and keep prices up by embargoes and trade barriers. If these don't work we have political power enough to get legislation that will impose discriminatory taxes on our competitors. And failing this we can always command a government subsidy for ourselves." Power-crazed *sisyphists*!

"Let's have Federal aid for projects to which we are unwilling to devote our own resources." Wasteful *sisyphists*!

"Let us have national unemployment compensation so, even if we do no work, we can get paid anyway." Money-mad *sisyphists*!

"Let us have wage, price, production, and exchange controls—eliminate market pricing as a guide to production and consumption—so that all may labor forever at posts assigned by government." Slavish *sisyphists*!

Enough of this. Each of us should make it his game to spot these persons who would magnify the effort required for a given result. They are to be found everywhere—on the farms, in pulpits and classrooms, in labor unions, in private offices, in governments and, alas, too often in the mirror. They are the friends of scarcity and the enemies of abundance. Antisocial *sisyphists*!

Let's make *sisyphism* a part of our mythology instead of our national policy!

21

EVIL BEGUN,
RARELY UNDONE

*In all things bad or evil, getting is
quicker and easier than getting rid
of them.*

—AUGUST HARE

A former aid to Franklin Roosevelt once told me how a
Congressman had presented to the President the "social security" idea. After listening to the proposal, the President
responded, "That is the silliest notion I have ever heard."
Ignoring the rebuff, the Congressman continued his plea.
According to my friend, the busy President finally closed the
interview: "Oh well, let's try it and see what happens."

Whether or not this is an accurate account, it is quite prob-
able that every step toward the planned economy and state
welfarism was, in its beginning, no more pretentious or popularly demanded than this. A single politician initiates the
scheme, gets it into Committee, works up a clamor, finds
lobbyists to push it until, sooner or later, it becomes the law
of the land.[1]

---

[1]Dr. Emerson Schmidt, eminent economist, discovered in his research
that in no instance has any one of the socialistic schemes been the result of
popular demand. See "The Public Demands . . .?" (*The Freeman*, August
1964).

"Social security" is an outstanding example of fiscal evil. Never in all history has there been a greater fraud, measured in money terms, than this. Private perpetrators of such chicanery would be imprisoned, and rightly. But evil once begun is with difficulty undone. The initial push behind this program—reckoned by energy expended—was certainly a tiny fraction of the energy exercised in opposition today. Yet, try now to wipe it from the statute books!

My purpose here is not to list all of these schemes—impossible—but rather to cite a few more examples and then examine why such legislation, easily initiated, is so difficult to abolish.

Reflect on the beginning of the Sixteenth Amendment, adopted in 1913. President Wilson and Cordell Hull spearheaded this enactment of the progressive income tax, one of the ten planks in the Communist Manifesto. The question is, how do we get rid of it?

Take two of President Hoover's programs: the Federal Farm Board and the Reconstruction Finance Corporation. True, they are no more. However, their removal was not because of any rejection of socialism. To the contrary, these were simply displaced by other programs, under other labels: government farm management and Federal financing on the grand scale. Replacing one intervention with something worse is no victory for freedom.

The Volstead Act—prohibition—passed in 1919, was abolished in 1933. If we knew why and how, we might use similar techniques to get rid of "social security" and thousands of other socialistic laws now in force.

The NIRA—wage, price and other controls—was a scheme dreamed up by a New England utility executive and urged upon President Franklin Roosevelt. The rescinding of this legislation may offer some lessons for us.

Another intervention, later abolished, was initiated by dairymen: oleomargarine manufacturers were prohibited from adding coloring to their product, lest it be made to look like butter. But it took years to be rid of this silly law.

What, then, do these few examples have to teach us?

The dairymen were facing competition from oleomargarine, a butter substitute. Technological advance in the refinement of animal and vegetable fats made it possible for mass-produced oleomargarine to sell below the price of butter. What to do? Simple: keep oleo from looking tasty by disallowing the coloring customarily added to butter! In a word, oleo, competitively good, must be made to look comparatively bad. Substitute disparagement for competition!

The lesson? The prohibition of oleo coloring was abolished because the fallacy of this dictocratic scheme was apparent to even casual thinkers. All of the anti-free market schemes now on the statute books—countless thousands of them—are just as fallacious as this prohibition and would also be abolished were their errors as apparent. Not casual but deeper thinking is the urgent requirement.

Most businessmen, with a few notable exceptions, favor competition for others but not themselves. Thus, the NIRA—National Industrial Recovery Act—was greeted with open arms as a way to be rid of dreaded competition. However, after a year or two of the "Blue Eagle" and its strangling controls, approval from the business community sharply declined. Businessmen went about their opposition cautiously, for it was a commonly held view that these controls had to be removed gradually or the economy would be thrown into a tailspin. Then one day the Supreme Court rendered its famous "Chicken Case" decision. Suddenly, all NIRA controls were abolished. Tailspin? Check the record. With the restoration of the market, all business activity showed an upward trend. Freedom works!

The lesson? The Supreme Court measured the NIRA against the Constitution, and found it out of line. Whatever shows forth on the political horizon, be it the original drafting of the Constitution or the latter-day ruling of the Supreme Court, is but a reflection of the leadership thinking of its period. Jefferson contended that there is a natural aristocracy among men—marked by virtue and talent. For a restoration of freedom—lifting of restrictions—no more is required than a restoration of a natural aristocracy—good thinkers who stand ramrod straight.

The prohibition against drinking was abolished for the same reason as the prohibition against oleo coloring: the fallacy was so obvious. Our experience with the Volstead Act has two vital lessons to teach: (1) that the substitution of governmental intervention for free market processes results in both economic and moral deterioration among producers, distributors, and consumers, and (2) that law has no function —none whatsoever—in the correction of moral deficiencies.

Following passage of this Act, what happened to the production of beer, wine, and liquor? Brought to an end? To the contrary, millions of people made "home brew," an inferior product, and homemade wine that was even worse; and, to top it off, "bathtub" gin! In addition, outlaws became manufacturers of this and that kind of "juice" which, in many instances, bordered on the poisonous.

What about distribution? Throughout the nation "speakeasies"—off-beat saloons—popped into existence. Bellhops, taxidrivers, and others became undercover merchants. Interestingly, one of today's best restaurants had its beginning as a "private club" for the elite, a dispenser of illegal beverages. From lawbreakers to free market makers!

What happened to the consumption of this inferior stuff? It is my guess that more alcohol was consumed than ever before. Illicit drinking becomes sportive, that is, people think it fun to play an out-guessing game, to defy and circumvent stupid laws; they appear to have no sense of wrongdoing when they break laws they believe to be doing wrong.

In any event, producers, distributors, and consumers became schemers, breakers of the law. As a consequence, they lost a great deal of respect for all law, even that which is appropriate.

Leave to the free market the production, distribution, and consumption of beverages—alcoholic or not—and all other peaceful trade in goods and services, without exception. This is lesson number one.

As to the second lesson, the law should be confined to codifying the taboos and intervening to prohibit any person's injury to others. It is none of government's business how or to what extent an individual injures himself. Injury to others is *the* societal problem, and this is the business of society's governmental agency. Injury to self, be it drug addiction or suicide, is strictly a personal problem and its remedy is to be achieved solely by self-correction.

If drunken drivers are killing others, the remedy is not to be found in outlawing alcohol. Penalize any driver for a crime he commits; this should discourage reckless driving, whatever the excuse. The fear of penalty and the widespread

habit of obeying the law suggests the limit of the influence
government can bring to bear against man's inhumanity to
man. To "outlaw" drunkenness or drug addiction is as fruitless as the legal prohibition of maniacal tendencies or sex
craze or the evil thoughts people entertain or any other psy-
chosis.

The obvious impossibility of correcting moral deficiencies
by force should be evidence enough to end such attempts.
Point to a single success! Those who sponsor and pass such
laws believe their job then is done when, indeed, it has not
begun; they have only put more laws on the statute books
which must, eventually and with enormous difficulty, be
abandoned—as was the Volstead Act, for instance.

There have, of course, been more repeals than the three
mentioned above. Another that comes to mind was President
Franklin Roosevelt's $25,000 annual salary limitation edict,
at the beginning of World War II. The reaction against it had
the force of a tidal wave. Why? It was so patently ridiculous!

Nonetheless, there are numerous equally ridiculous, socialistic laws now on the statute books. Why, then, are they not
repealed? Why the difficulty?

A major part of the difficulty, it seems, is the fact that a
bad scheme, once enacted into the law of the land, spawns
and develops a vested interest in its preservation.

The most effective opposition to the repeal of Prohibition
came from the bootleggers and their tribe.

Why is not the government's unemployment insurance program abandoned? By now, millions have a vested interest in
its continuance: those who prefer getting paid for not working
rather than competing for a job.

Who stood out most tenaciously against NIRA's demise?

As in ever so many other cases, the enormous bureaucracy which had a vested interest in NIRA forever: snappy jobs at good pay!

The vested interest in "social security" and countless other laws is now beyond comprehension.

But in the final analysis, vested interests, however powerful, cannot withstand the light of understanding. When the fallacies of laws are apparent even to casual observers, such laws are abandoned. But the fallacies of most socialistic measures are not easily detected; casual onlookers are taken in by them. When enough of us can see that antitrust laws are denying competition in the name of protecting competition, the antitrust laws will as readily fall by the wayside as did the inept Volstead Act.

My barber was complaining about high prices. I explained inflation and its cause: excessive costs of government brought on by state welfarism and interventionism. I argued that there would be no halt to rising prices until these causes were removed.

"How and when can we stop these?"

"When you start!"

"Start what?"

"Start thinking for yourself!"

Here is the point: That barber has more common sense than the dictocrats who are denying his freedom. Except that he does not realize this! There are countless millions just like him, whose liberation is simply a matter of waking up, coming to themselves—unmasking.

This is the way and, in my view, the only way to change from evil coercive collectivism to the virtuous and voluntary practice of freedom.

22

THE GLORY OF WORK

*All growth depends upon activity.
There is no development physically
or intellectually without effort, and
effort means work. Work is not a
curse; it is the prerogative of intelligence, the only means to manhood, and the measure of civilization.*

—CALVIN COOLIDGE

Decoration Day always came on May 30 when I was a boy, whether the date fell on Saturday or Sunday or any weekday. There was a procession led by a flag-bearer, followed by a fife-and-drum corps, uniformed Civil War veterans carrying muskets, and town dignitaries. The graves were decorated, a gun salute over each, a prayer and, always, a patriotic speech. Impressionable youngsters tagged along in admiration.

Times have changed. Hardly anyone today recalls the origin of Decoration Day or thinks of a veteran—North or South—who gave his life for this or that "purpose."

In our time, Memorial Day, Washington's birthday, and other national holidays are on Monday. They are mere excuses for lengthened weekends, attempts to get away from it all. They must be linked to the retirement syndrome—an escape from the effort of earning a living. This calls for an examination of our attitudes toward work.

As I see it, the purpose of earthly life is growth in awareness, perception, consciousness. The means to this noble objective is work, which includes a constant striving for achievement along the line of one's uniqueness—fiddler, fisherman, poet, golfer, sculptor, or whatever.

Why glorify work? By and large, it is looked upon as an *unfortunate* necessity, something to escape from, to avoid if at all possible. Instead of accepting work and ever more work as the vital means to every aim of life, most people aspire to shorter hours, vacations, retirement, getting out of rather than into life—in a word, vegetation.

An economist of a prestigious businessman's organization shares this commonly held view:

> The most that can be said for work is that it is an unfortunate necessity.

I am reminded of a comparable statement by a noted sociologist: "Government is a necessary evil." Not so, I contend. Anything that is necessary to the attainment of intellectual, moral, and ethical ends is neither evil nor unfortunate, be it government or work.

Why the common tendency to look upon work as a curse and do as little of it as possible? What is the enormous price of this error? These are the questions I wish to examine.

Conceded, there is one sense in which any given individual might properly try to avoid certain kinds of work. For instance, the work that most attracts me has to do with the freedom way of life—an ever-improving understanding and exposition of it. Thus, I prefer not to be a carpenter, a food raiser or merchant; let others be insurance or real estate salesmen, builders of autos or roads, makers of clothes or desks or pencils. The free economy tends to match jobs to persons who have unique talents for them; "to each his own." The realization of my hope in my job rests on division of labor and unfettered exchange, that is, on a society in which I can exchange my speciality for other specializations. Freeing me to be me and, by the same token, releasing you to be you! This, in an economic sense, is what the freedom philosophy is all about.

While it is sound practice to avoid certain *kinds* of work, all will agree that work is a necessity—for the rule in reality is to work or perish. No argument! The point at issue has to do with one's attitude toward his work. Is it a fortunate opportunity or an unfortunate necessity? Were the matter put to vote, I expect the "unfortunates" would have it by a mile. Few are those who would rather work than play, who prefer being on the job to goofing off.

Today, too many individuals look upon their work not as a joyous employment of their time but, rather, as sheer drudgery—a pain in the neck, a curse instead of a blessing. And note that those who regard their work as an unfortunate necessity are not confined to any given job level. Many highly placed corporate executives are as anxious for retirement as window cleaners are anxious for a 20-hour week. This escapism from presumed drudgery seems to infect all categories of workers.

There is a price exacted for thinking of work as an unfortunate necessity, as a curse. The millions of individuals who have this attitude are vulnerable to exploitation. And there is no shortage of exploiters, of those who are ready and eager to take advantage of this erroneous way of thinking about work. This shortsighted attitude toward work underlies the coercive power over the economy exercised by labor unions. In the absence of this attitude, labor unions would possess no more coercive power than a chamber of commerce, a Ladies Aid Society, or these thoughts of mine.

What is the labor union's stock in trade? Shorter work weeks, more vacations and holidays, above-market wages; in a word, more and more affluence for less and less effort. Such tactics appeal only to those who look upon work as an unfortunate necessity, never to those who love their work. Are such persons comprised solely of waiters or dishwashers or street cleaners? Indeed, not! According to the evidence, the labor union theme appeals to policemen, teachers, engineers, electricians, plumbers, airline pilots, to a thousand and one occupations—some of them highly paid, indeed.

Above-market wages and below-market hours create unemployment. The government, under union pressure, picks up the tab by make-work projects—urban renewal, moon shots, ad infinitum—adding billions of dollars annually to the costs of government. The costs that cannot be met by direct tax levies are met by increasing the money supply: inflation. Prices rise as the dollar buys less and less. Who suffers most? The relatively poor, the very individuals these tactics are supposed to be helping!

He who deplores the ever-rising cost of living should look to the source: the ever-diminishing love of work.

There is yet another price we pay, perhaps the highest of all. There are those at every level who love their work. However, if theirs happens to be an occupation monopolized by labor unions, they have no choice but to join the antiwork parade or to go jobless and hungry or to go on the dole. Thus, as the repugnance for work increases, it taxes and tends to bury initiative, incentive, ingenuity and ambition under the general decadence. The exemplars of sound thinking diminish. What a price this is!

The remedy for all of this is, of course, self-respect, the pride of achievement, the urge to excel, the love of work. However, this is a problem that each individual must wrestle with personally. Whether one cultivates an attitude of love or of hate toward the things and the persons involved in his life is strictly a subjective matter. Anyone who has a modicum of self-determination can, if he so wills it, displace his hatred and spitefulness with love—including the love or glorification of work. Here is an excellent and helpful observation by William Osler, M.D.:

> Though little, the master word looms large in meaning. It is the "open sesame" to every portal, the great equalizer, the philosopher's stone which transmutes all base metal of humanity into gold. The stupid it will make bright, the bright brilliant, and the brilliant steady. To youth it brings hope, to the middle-aged confidence, to the aged repose. It is directly responsible for all advances in medicine during the past 25 years. Not only has it been the touchstone of progress, but it is the measure of success in everyday life. And the master word is *work*.

If one grasps Dr. Osler's point, and particularly if one is interested in the development or emergence of self, then work will be embraced—loved—as the means to these lofty ends. He will discover that there is no better prescription for good health and long life than joyous work.

Another distinguished physician, Dr. Hans Selye, names several famous men who lived to a ripe old age, and adds this comment:

> Of course, in their many years of intense activity, these people never "worked": they lived a life of "leisure" by working at what they liked to do.[1]

"What they liked to do"! With such fortunate ones there is no problem. They have hit upon their distinctive energies and talents, either by accident or by self-discovery. Let me illustrate.

We have a private garbage collector—a one-man, one-truck enterprise. He remarked one day while emptying a can of garbage, "Mr. Read, I just love my work." He would not love my work nor I his, any more than I would love being President of U. S. Steel or of the U.S.A.

Granted, millions have never discovered their uniqueness and thus labor at tasks they look upon as drudgery. For what they may be worth, I have two suggestions for these people:

1. Reflect on your work until you discover reasons for enjoying it; learn to love whatever your engagement with life might be.
2. If you cannot do this, switch jobs! For pride in your work is the first step toward joy in your life. In a word, find out what your uniqueness is and go to it. Excel!

Wrote Henry Giles: "Man must work. That is certain as

---

[1]See a splendid article, "But Hard Work Isn't Bad For You" by Dr. Hans Selye. *Reader's Digest,* June 1973.

the sun. But he may work grudgingly or he may work gratefully; he may work as a man, or he may work as a machine. There is no work so rude, that he may not exalt it; no work so impassive, that he may not breathe a soul into it; no work so dull that he may not enliven it."

My own work intrigues me more and more each year. I could wish you no greater blessings than such joy in whatever task engages you.

23

EMPLOYMENT REDEFINED

Just definitions either prevent or
put an end to disputes.
—NATHANIEL EMMONS

The preceding chapter includes this observation: "Above-market wages and below-market hours cause unemployment." One of the best economic thinkers of my acquaintance suggested: "'Below-market hours' should be deleted. Hardly anyone will know what you mean, for nearly everybody believes that shorter work weeks make for the employment of more people." Conceded, this is the common belief and, further, it is a correct view if "employment" be defined as "job occupancy."[1]

Here are my contentions: (1) If employment be properly defined, then any deviation from the free market—whether above-market wages or below-market hours—causes unemployment; and, (2) employment thought of as no more than mere job occupancy leads inevitably to Marxian socialism.

---

[1] The figures on employment and unemployment reported by the Bureau of Labor Statistics refer only to job occupancy.

These would seem to be reasons enough to reflect on the use of the word "employment."

How should employment be defined, that is, if the term is to make any sense? Here is my answer: *Employment is job occupancy free of all coercive elements.* The opposite is job occupancy free of all voluntary elements. If this distinction is not made no one can tell the difference between full employment and full enslavement.

Were the market 100 per cent free there would be no involuntary unemployment, which is to say that full employment would obtain. Why? Because there is always more work to be done than there are persons to do it. The situation of full employment obtains when any employer may exchange *his* proffered wage with any employee for *his* proffered service. The terms are mutually agreeable or there would be no deal. In the event of no deal, the unemployment would be voluntary.

If the society were 100 per cent coercive there would be no voluntary employment. Instead of full employment there would be full enslavement.

Neither of these 100 per cent situations has ever existed; both have been approximated. The free market has been approximated in the U.S.A., England, Hong Kong. The nearest approximations to the coercive society are to be found in Russia, China, Cuba, Chile.

Now to my point. When we think of employment solely as job occupancy then there is no distinction between jobs freely chosen and jobs coercively imposed. If full employment be anyone's goal, and if employment means no more than job occupancy, then Russia's coercive system is superior. Why? There is no "unemployment" there! Even women are compelled to work in the fields or at other dictocratic assignments. The man who, if he had his choice, would play the piccolo, is assigned to the sputnik factory, and so on. In Russia, it is "do as we say" or Siberia—or worse!

Merely reflect on how inane it is to label a freely chosen job the same as a coercively imposed one, referring to both forms of labor as "employment"! The only terms that make sense are employment and enslavement respectively.

I have asserted that neither situation has ever completely obtained, that is, neither freedom nor coercion has or ever will be 100 per cent practiced. Even in Russia there is a great deal of free choice. Collective farm hands have their private plots where they can raise what they please and sell for whatever they can get. Talented athletes, dancers, singers are permitted to pursue their uniqueness. In a word, using my definition, there is some employment in Russia; it is not all enslavement.

And even in the U.S.A. there is some coercion; indeed, it is growing rapidly. In this land of ours there is much employment and, let us confess, there is a growing enslavement.

Growing enslavement! The essence of enslavement is coercion and it matters not where or how it interferes with the voluntary market processes. In Russia, for example, most of the people have no more choice than slaves. The coercion is head-on! In the U.S.A., on the other hand, it takes devious rather than direct forms. For instance, I use the socialized mail "service." Others are forced to make up the difference between the high cost and my subsidized price, thus enslaving them to that extent. Coercion, often indirect, disrupts market choices at millions of points rather than directly and all at once.

These indirect enslavements tend to fool me; they make me feel freer than I really am. Nonetheless, I am enslaved in some measure; I am forced to contribute toward the numerous subsidies granted by government to people and programs not of my choice. To the extent of the coercion, regardless of how devious, to that extent do Americans move away from full employment and toward full enslavement. The coercive control of people's lives, be it in the form of wage and price controls, political manipulation of money and credit, or whatever, is really nothing less than slavery. It just seems less; which explains, in no small measure, why most of us are so easily "taken in."

Now to my contention that below-market hours cause unemployment. The vital issue, as I see it, is whether or not a man is in control of himself. Is he in charge of his own life, or does someone own him? What this boils down to is the market method of determining wages and other conditions of employment, versus the compulsory method (socialism, dictatorship, slavery, closed shop, or whatever else it may be called).

It seems to me that "below-market hours" is merely an equivalent term for "above-market wages." Suppose that the market rate of wages is $2.00 an hour: demanding $2.00 for only 12 minutes work is the same as demanding $10.00 an hour. Unless a man is free to price his services competitively in the market, he is not in control of himself; someone else owns him. If he willingly accepts the terms of the contract, it is employment; if not, it is enslavement.

My second contention: If a significant number of people confuse employment with mere job occupancy, there will be a diminished resistance to the drift toward enslavement.

I have already suggested that coercion is socialism's hall-mark. And it matters not how or when it insinuates itself into the economy—whether open and obvious as in Russia, or screened and obscure as in this country. Note well, therefore, that every year, since the late twenties, the U.S.A. has been moving closer and closer to Marxian socialism—dictocratic control over people's lives. This is a fact. And there is the accompanying fact that nearly everyone thinks of employment as nothing more than a guaranteed wage—which is to say that popular understanding of the free market is nearly nil. Taken together, these two facts add up to our present predicament.

True, no one, here or elsewhere, occupies a job free of all coercive influence. However, we can bear in mind that one is truly employed only to the extent that he is free—his own man. Otherwise, nothing can save him from the plunge into socialism.

24

HOW TO STOP INFLATION

To know truly is to know by causes.
—FRANCIS BACON

How to stop inflation? Remove the cause! Stopping inflation is as simple and as difficult as that. Everyone says he's against inflation; yet, what do we find? Nearly everyone overlooking the sole remedy and, instead, conjuring up schemes to soften inflation's disastrous effects. Interestingly, all schemes or nostrums which ignore the cause, if and when adopted, sink us ever deeper into the mire. As if inflation weren't bad enough, most proffered "cures" would worsen the situation!

Many years ago a professor of economics told a group of us about his experiences at the University of Heidelberg during the German inflation. Faculty members were paid once a month. As the inflation began to gallop, they were paid twice a month, then each week, then each day. Finally, they were paid in the morning, rushing the checks home to their *Frauen* before going to their classrooms. Why? Prices were multiplying many times each day, so shop in the morning! There came a time—August 1923—when 100 billion marks would not buy a loaf of bread.

What was this professor's recommendation to those in our group who foresaw similar problems in our own country? His advice was to out-produce inflation! Imagine a professor of economics not understanding that all production creates its own purchasing power!

A few thoughts inspired by the professor's naive thinking: Production involves the efficient combination and use of scarce resources, in the process paying for each resource a price high enough to pull it away from other owners and other uses. To produce more housing, for instance, involves paying higher wages, higher prices for lumber, hardware, masonry, and the like, to attract those scarce resources from other uses. Meanwhile, each supplier of such resources has the additional income to spend, a process sometimes expressed as Say's Law: "Production creates its own purchasing power."

The truth is that inflation does not result from the lack of housing or other goods or services. It is nothing more nor less than the printing of what the government has declared to be legal tender, that is, printing ever-increasing quantities of fiat money. Unless house-building or other productive activities stop those printing presses—an absurdity—then trying to out-produce inflation is as futile as trying to out-run one's own shadow. So the professor's cure is on a level with most remedies now being dinned into our ears.

It is not that the inventors of these schemes agree with inflation. Quite the contrary! Rather, it is that they see no way to be rid of it; inflation is here to stay—even worsen—thus,

why not find a way to prosper and thrive in a monetary holo-
caust! The fact that this requires nonexistent skills in legerdemain deters them not.

Two such schemes recently have come to my attention. The
first proposes that all contracts—loans, for instance—be repaid (legally enforced) in dollars of the same purchasing
value as when contracted. If the value of the dollar should decline at the rate of 15 per cent a year, then a 10-year loan of
a thousand dollars would be repaid in the amount of more
than $5,000, plus interest.

Even in the face of the current inflationary pattern, what
borrower would be willing to sign such a contract? Only the
person who cannot see "beyond the end of his nose." There
would be little if any futures trading; indeed, contractual
relations would all but cease, production would decline at a
frightening rate. Further, there is nothing in this scheme to
halt the outpouring of fiat money; it would go on its merry
way and, because of the fall off in production, the dollar
would buy far less than were the scheme never adopted.
Approval? Indeed, not!

The other scheme requires that all business ventures be
compelled to adopt the "profit-sharing" procedure—employees as well as entrepreneurs sharing in the gains. This is
inspired by some remarkable successes such as Lincoln Electric of Cleveland. The assumption is that if Jim Lincoln could,
by this arrangement, earn a great deal for himself, pay higher
wages than others, and undersell all of his competitors, so
could everyone else—hundreds of thousands of businessmen
from hamburger stand owners to General Motors. Simply
pass a law and make every entrepreneur operate like Mr.
Lincoln!

Overlooked is the fact that only one Jim Lincoln ever existed. There are no two entrepreneurs who operate their businesses alike, nor could they do so if they tried. Each is novel to some extent; and consumers—that's all of us—are thus advantaged.

Any profit-sharing arrangement should, in all fairness, be also a loss-sharing arrangement. But most wage earners would shy away from any employer who required employees to share any losses his business might incur. Why? Tens of thousands of businesses fail annually, as everyone knows.

Were profit sharing made compulsory for everyone, production would dramatically decline, just as in the first scheme. There would be other results, no less disastrous.

Out-producing inflation or fulfilling contracts at a constant purchasing power or forcing every business to engage in profit sharing are no more than "pipe dreams." Adoption need not be feared. These schemes merely illustrate how people avoid pinpointing the cause of inflation and, thus, propose remedies which compound the problem.

However, what do we find in the day-to-day world of "practical" politics? The worst of all possible schemes: price control and rationing as edicts by the Federal government and wage controls in the hands of labor unions. Below-market prices and above-market wages! Inflation is not questioned; we have instead only futile attempts to escape the effects, which make the effects increasingly disastrous. In what way? Production is both diminished and distorted. Figuring out how to outscheme the political schemers takes the place of discovering how best to satisfy consumer preferences. Schemers with political and coercive power make schemers of every one of us they overpower.

To illustrate: By reason of governmental intervention, the supply of gas and oil is curbed and the demand increased. What to do? Ration the fuel! To the station attendant say, "Fill 'er up." "Sorry, only $3 worth to a person." So the car owner takes what he can get and goes to another station repeating, "Fill 'er up." Gas wasted going from station to station! Eventually, all the gas is gone, but consumers still have "gas money" burning holes in their pockets. The best way to ration gas or any other scarce resource is to let the price rise to a point where the supply is sufficient to meet the demand.

We need only come to our senses to stop inflation; nothing is required beyond discovering its cause and then being rid of it. The cause? *Overextended government.* To repeat what many of us have written over and over again: when the costs of government rise beyond the point where it is no longer politically expedient to defray the costs by direct tax levies, governments all over the world resort to an expansion of paper money—inflation—as a means of making up the difference. Inflation dilutes and depreciates the medium of exchange as a means of siphoning private property into the coffers of government. Here we have the cause, so simple to to see through. But being rid of the cause is not simple. Why the difficulty?

The difficulty is rooted in an unintelligent interpretation of self-interest. Today, all of us without exception are feeding more or less at the Federal trough. True, there are a few who are force-fed, not dipping into the trough willingly. Finding it necessary to live in the world as it is, they participate in the deficit-burdened, socialistic mail system—to name but one of many examples. But most citizens today—a number perilously approaching 100 per cent—mistakenly feel that they have a vested interest in the continuance of one or more, if not all, Federal "programs" that go to make up the deficits that can be met only by inflation: fiat money made possible by legal tender laws.

Perhaps this citizen only wishes to be paid for not farming, another to receive social security or Medicare, still others to be protected against competition, or to have their education subsidized, or a Gateway Arch for their home town, or whatever. It would take a book just to list the titles of all the Federal handouts and discriminatory edicts.[1] Anyway, count the persons you know who completely ignore the "gravy train," who would concede nothing to government beyond a peace-keeping, justice-dispensing agency of society, who are free from the feeling that they have a vested interest in this or that deficit-creating, political gimmick. They are "as rare as hens' teeth!"

If an individual could perfectly identify how his self-interest is best served, he would be all-wise. However, I am not alluding to perfect wisdom but to that level of intelligence any adolescent should possess. Most youngsters know that their self-interest is not advanced by stealing—living off the fruits of the labor of others coercively exacted. They would not regard face-to-face thievery as in their own interest. And there are thousands of high school students who are bright enough to see that there is no distinction between pointing the gun oneself and getting the Federal government to do the "stick up." The loot would be ill-gained in either case. Self-

---

[1]See *Encyclopedia of U.S. Government Benefits,* a tome of more than 1,000 pages with over 10,000 "benefits." (Union City, N.J.: Wm. H. Wise and Co., Inc., 1965.)

interest is not served by either method. One need not be overly brilliant to see this.

Yet, what do we find? Millions upon millions identifying self-interest with legal plunder! The more political largess they can get—regardless of the force used—the better. It is not that these people, many of whom are college graduates, could not rise above this infantile level of thinking; they could if they would, but they don't. Further, these millions do not see how their self-interest is subverted rather than served by this socialistic plundering, and they cannot be expected to understand why inflation is not also identified with their self-interest. They see inflation, if they see at all, as the means of filling the thousands of troughs from which they feed without either thought or effort. They love the role of parasites!

Given these millions who thoughtlessly behave this way, plus the political exploiters of nonsense, the situation, on the surface at least, looks hopeless. Stopping inflation appears to be impossible, and certainly this would be the case were it a numbers problem. But, thank heavens, it never has been a numbers problem, is not now, nor will it ever be. It is strictly a matter of inspired and intelligent leadership.

Statesmen—in and out of office—are more and more in evidence, persons who think for themselves and stand forthright for their enlightened convictions. These few—thousands, of course—understand that self-interest is to be identified with individuals in the role of hosts—producers, not parasites. They also know that inflation is deadly—for parasites cannot exist without hosts. As the troughs empty, attrition increases, especially among the parasites.

As this natural aristocracy—comprised of men of virtue and

talents—approaches the pink of condition, rises to the top in thinking how self-interest is best served, the nonsense is stopped dead, then subsides! Your role and mine? Try one's best to be this kind of an exemplary aristocrat. This, I submit, is the sole formula to stop inflation.

25

HOW NOT TO BE OWNED

The man who is not permitted to
own is owned.

—SANTAYANA

There would be no tigers in zoos were they to remain as ferocious as when first captured. But once owned, they soon become docile.

Human slavery is an ancient institution in all parts of the globe. Slavery would not exist, however, if captives remained as intractable as when first shanghaied by slave traders. But once owned, they become complacent.

Airlift a family from Omaha and the next day install them as citizens of Omsk. The sudden contrast would make them furious but, once owned, they would soon become as unaware of their plight as are most Russians today.

Similarly, with our fellow citizens. Reflect on the increased take of the people's property by government since say 1913.[1]

---

[1]For example, Federal government expenditures were $1 billion in 1913. Today they approximate $250 billion.

Had this enormous increase been imposed all at once, the political perpetrators would have been unseated just as promptly. But let the increase be imposed gradually, as during the past sixty years, and the deterioration of private ownership is greeted indifferently, if not with approval.

All of recorded history reveals a struggle to achieve selfhood, including its corollary, ownership of property—control of one's own. Who is to control the fruits of your labor, you or others? Wars have been fought and governments have been shaped to resolve this question. Private ownership is the very heart of the free society but its establishment and practice have been sporadic at best. Throughout the ages, the plunderers have had it by a mile, not only in primitive societies but also in the modern U.S.A. Private ownership comes out in last place.

In my view, the losing concept is right and the winning notion is and always has been wrong. In the light of all that has been written over the centuries in support of private ownership, why is it in last rather than in first place? Why has the rationale of selfhood—to each his own—failed so miserably, as if it were an incomprehensible concept? There has to be an explanation; this is my attempt to find it.

The answer, as I see it, was revealed three thousand years ago when the Ten Commandments were first recorded. The Commandment, "Thou shalt not steal," presupposes private ownership. Why? How possibly could anything be stolen were it not first owned!

Here we have a stress on the importance of private ownership, so strong that a violation was deemed a religious offense. There was, however, a blind spot in this belief which led to its violation on the grand scale. The blind spot? Human slavery was an accepted, and even an honored institution among the very people who gave us this Commandment, who thought of it as "pure gospel." To own slaves, openly accepted! To be owned, blindly approved!

What comes to light in this blatant contradiction? The all but hidden answer to the private ownership dilemma: Millions hold private ownership as a sacred right for themselves but fail to realize that *unless this precise right is extended to everyone else, it is no right at all*—a mere fiction! When each citizen proclaims ownership of his earnings and fails to grant respect, and insist upon a similar ownership on the part of everyone else, the outcome has to be all citizens against one. For the person who is not permitted to own what he has earned is in fact owned by a master!

Let us not poke too much fun at the ancient Israelites for their queer notions of right and wrong, each respecting his own property but not that of the other person. Each, to them, meant mostly I, rarely you!

How different are present-day Americans? Perhaps 999 out of every thousand, be they politicians, welfare statists, or whoever, actually believe that they have a right to the fruits of their own labor. Try to take their income dollars from them face-to-face and watch this belief assert itself!

But, as with the Israelites, there may not be more than one in a thousand today who will accord the person and the property of others the same respect he accords his own. Thus, in these loose terms, the odds are a thousand to one against private ownership as a working principle. And simply because nearly everyone defends only his own right to private ownership which, of course, leaves the institution defenseless.

Take what is obviously the opposite to private ownership,

namely, human slavery as popularly understood. Ask Joe Doakes or whoever, "Do you favor or disapprove?" Most Americans would scoff at a question which so grievously affronts their sanity. The reason? They think of human slavery as only a Simon Legree-Uncle Tom relationship, a white with a lash compelling a black to do his bidding.

Now pose this question: do you approve or disapprove of the compulsion which forces the piccolo player to labor in the sputnik factory? People's "sanity" will be less affronted. After all, it is the government, not a mean, self-seeking villain doing the compelling! But, really, what is the difference between a political collective backed by a constabulary and a man's passion to enslave backed by a lash? There is no less compulsion in one case than in the other. Neither Uncle Tom nor the piccolo player owns his life. It is slavery in either case.

Go next to the still less obvious, and ask: do you approve or disapprove the forcible taking of everyone's income in the nation to finance shall we say the Gateway Arch? Here "sanity" is hardly affronted at all. As tigers in a zoo, most people have adapted themselves to their spoon-fed habitat and have become docile. Yet, this is enslavement no less than that imposed by Simon Legree.

It is as simple as this: If a man has a right to his life—to "own" himself—it logically follows that he has a right to sustain his life, the sustenance of life being the fruits of one's own labor. Thus, to the extent that one's sustenance is taken, to that extent is life taken—to that extent is one owned instead of owning himself.

Where lies the remedy? What has to happen before individuals will concede to others precisely the same right to ownership as they seek for themselves? Observe the Golden

Rule? Yes, that is the answer all right, but in the same sense that "Thou shalt not steal" is the answer.

Here is a realization we must come to: The Golden Rule and the Commandment are but labels for ideal and hoped-for relationships. In a dictocratic society they are unattainable pipe dreams. In a free society they automatically exist. These ideal relationships grow toward reality only to the extent that the free society approaches reality. This is to say that freedom and private ownership, as well as an observation of the Golden Rule, rise or fall in unison; they are inseparably linked!

Once this is understood, it becomes clear why "Thou shalt not steal" has so little practical meaning among people who permit some men to own other men. People who view human slavery, in any of its numerous forms, as an acceptable institution have no inkling of the free society. The Commandment against theft is no more than a mystical aspiration in a dictocratic situation, and cannot be otherwise.

Whenever the right to the fruits of one's own labor is gaining acceptance and respect it will be seen that an understanding of the free society is likewise gaining. Of course, the reverse is true. When state welfarism and government control is on the rampage, as in the U.S.A. today, be it noted that there are leaders by the tens of thousands from all walks of life—business, education, religion, and so on—who wave aside the free society as a viable way of life. They are leading us down the road to serfdom and, interestingly enough, are unaware of their mischief. Their philosophy, though never in these realistic terms, is that you and I shall not be permitted to own; we are to be owned. And so are they—though they know it not.

The above is a long introduction to a brief conclusion: The coercive control of people's lives—including the fruits of their labor—falls or rises precisely as the practice of freedom increases or wanes, which is to say, as authoritarianism relaxes or tightens its grip.

Freedom is the right of anyone to do anything, so long as it is peaceful. Government is freedom's peace-keeping agency; its role is limited to codifying and prohibiting all unpeaceful or destructive activities.

Given this freedom arrangement, each citizen is free to produce anything he pleases, to exchange on mutually agreeable terms with whomever he pleases, to do as he chooses with what is his own and without trespass against others.

We have in this ideal situation only willing exchanges, whether of goods or services. Each citizen gains in his own judgment or he would not make the exchanges. Each owns; no one is owned. There is neither thievery nor enslavement; both are impossible. Each is behaving toward others as he would have them behave toward him. In a word, the Golden Rule is observed as freedom is practiced.

How to own rather than be owned? Learn the freedom philosophy and how to live by it!

26

IF I WERE KING

No man is wise enough, nor good enough, to be trusted with unlimited powers.

—CALEB C. COLTON

To imagine I were king is pure fiction, merely suggestive, for my first act would be to abdicate. Kingship is not my cup of tea.

Perhaps a better caricature of omnipotence would be a genie—as the actress in the TV show, "I Dream of Jeannie." She simply folds her arms, makes a wish, and blinks her eyes. Presto! The wish instantly becomes the reality.

The question I am pondering is this: If I possessed such power, would I use it to rid the world of all I believe to be evil? For instance, what of these few specifics among the thousand and one forms of human behavior I deplore:

1. War, murder, thievery, slavery?
2. Dictatorial know-it-all-ness?
3. Medicare, "social security," and similar welfare programs?
4. Control of prices by government and of wages by labor unions?

5. Government in such businesses as mail delivery and education?

I have listed these samplings in the reverse order of their popularity or public acceptance. Nearly everyone deplores war, murder, thievery, human slavery. There is a common desire to be rid of these evils. But note how the popular attitude changes as we move down the list: common acceptance instead of rejection by the time we have reached "social security."

The point is this: I would be applauded were I to use my magic power to do away with murder, but roundly condemned were I to eliminate government "education," though the latter seems unprincipled and impractical to me.

On what forms of behavior, then, would I fold my arms, make a wish, and blink my eyes? *Not one, not even murder!*

I aspire exclusively to those forms of power which I readily concede to all other human beings. What may they be? The power to exercise and improve my own faculties, to grow intellectually, morally, spiritually. What power will I not willingly concede to any other person and—by the same token—refuse to use myself? The power to interfere with or to control in any respect the *creative activities* of anyone, whoever or wherever he may be. The lack of such power simply leaves me in my place, makes a noninterfering citizen of me, forces me to attend to my own business.

Suppose I could eliminate murder and all else which seems evil to me through a simple wish. In that case, according to my principle of universality, I would have to concede that identical power of legerdemain to everyone else. What would be the result?

Everyone would direct his magic against his pet dislikes.

So certain are millions of people about their panaceas for a perfect world, and so varying are their nostrums, that every societal institution would be erased from the face of the earth! Not only would murder, wars, thievery, slavery be at an end, but so would everything else—mail delivery, private or public; education, private or public; business, private or public; churches, catholic or protestant. Certainly, man and all his institutions would disappear—perhaps the entire planet!

Return to mankind as he now exists and to the world as it is—with no genies among us. But if that power were possessed, would it be used? Yes, and by millions of people. How can one be so certain of this? By observing what these millions do in the absence of this magic power: they resort to coercion to get their way! Unable to reform others by a blink of the eyes, they try to implant their "wisdom" by physical force—"Do as we say, or else!" They seize the police power of government and use it to serve their devious and contradictory ends—frustrated genies with guns!

If these coercionists could work their will upon others by blinking their eyes, would they do so? Of course, and with the aforementioned disastrous results. To the extent that they get their way by coercion, to that same extent is disaster inflicted upon mankind, as we can readily observe all about us.

Those who condemn the use of coercion must be cautious lest they condemn themselves in the process, so general is the domineering trait. One meets these persons on every hand and in all walks of life. Ever so many would rule our lives if they could; all they lack is the political power. I have learned not to argue with these self-designated miracle workers; I just don't drink tea with them.

As to those who have gained power and do in fact control

our lives, what can one do in opposition beyond setting a better example? You and I can try to understand and explain why we would not wave either the magic wand or the policeman's club. We can demonstrate why it is both immoral and impractical to even hope for a free lunch or to wish that others might be carbon copies of ourselves. For anyone to hold such power over others, as I see it, is an absolute contradiction of the Cosmic Plan.

If we want "two chickens in every pot," we must learn to raise more and better chickens with less effort. Similarly, with all the goods, services, and ideas we desire. Learn to overcome by excelling, this being the sole means to individual growth. If another's way of life is superior to mine, let him demonstrate it to the point where I can grasp the truth he perceives. Let him explain in terms I can understand. By so doing, he grows—and perhaps I will. But to coercively impose his way upon me is to stunt both his growth and mine. This attempt at lording it over others is characteristic of little folks foolishly trying to play God. I share this conclusion from the *Journal Intimé* of Amiel:

I have never been able to see any necessity for imposing myself upon others.

And so, if I were king, I would renounce the throne. This would free me from the baleful superstition that mine is a "Divine Right" to rule and, at the same time, leave others free to live their own lives.

27
THE RIGHT TO QUIT

Man, proud man! dressed in a little
brief authority, plays such fantastic
tricks before high heaven as make
the angels weep.

—SHAKESPEARE

Were a child not allowed to graduate out of kindergarten he would never know fifth-grade arithmetic. Were the government to freeze you in your present employment, the world of opportunity would forever be closed to you. Am I conjuring up fantasies? Indeed, not! Occurrences similar to these are common, and they are coercively decreed by "man, proud man," in ways "as make the angels weep."

The government of Libya has issued a decree expropriating 51 per cent control of all foreign oil companies. Among the provisions:

All employees of the affected concerns are required to continue to work and none "may resign his position" without government permission regardless of the worker's nationality. Punishment by fine or imprisonment is provided for anyone acting contrary to the decree.[1]

Several American companies are involved, one having 165 U.S. citizens on their payroll in Libya. Suppose you were one of these and wanted to quit your job in that far-off land and return to your own country. Could you do so? Only with the permission of unsympathetic bureaucrats!

Shocking? Yes, indeed, but it is "par for the course," in line with the politico-economic trends of our day, here and elsewhere. There may be contractual obligations to fulfill, of course, which mandate a continued association; but beyond that, what is the difference between the forcible denial of the right to quit the job one has and the forcible denial of the right to start a job one wants? It is violence in either case and he who condones the latter cannot logically look unfavorably upon the former. Indeed, the supporters of violence in any area should, if consistent, welcome violence in all areas and places, even the forcible denial of the right to quit a job, whether in Libya, or Russia, or Hometown, USA.

Take an entrepreneur whose business is unionized and who may want your services; you, in turn, wish to work for him. Who has the say-so? Not the businessman, not you, but the union. Or, let us say that you are a member of a union that has gone on strike, whereas you do not wish to quit. Your wish is but a dream!

Let us not, however, confine our criticism to unions and job control. There is no distinction between control of jobs and control of goods. Thus, all who favor wage and price controls are on the side of violence—coercive denial of your

---

[1] *The Wall Street Journal,* September 10, 1973, p. 32.

right and mine to deal with whomsoever we please in free and willing exchange. Neither they nor coercionists in any other field can make the case against the Libyan decree or against holding children forever in kindergarten. They have disqualified themselves!

The right to quit is fully as important as the right to start. To deny any man either of these rights is to deny him his right to life. It is to freeze him into his position regardless of how ill-chosen it might be and to erect a barrier to opportunities irrespective of the wonderful promises they may hold. It is to immobilize and stop the growth of an erstwhile living human being. Making things out of humans is inhuman!

Who, pray tell, are these makers of things out of human beings? They are those "dressed in a little brief authority," those who acquire power and then lord it over us. They are the ones who are unaware of how little they know, who know not how to quit their meddlesome intervention.

Use the right phrasing and even these authoritarians would ridicule such behavior. How many of them, for instance, would buy the "Divine Right of Kings" theory that had its heyday during the reign of James I? I have not met one in my time. Yet, in what respect do they differ? They no more question their competency to rule than did that egotistic monarch of an age unenlightened in freedom.

In the preceding chapter, first published as an article, I said: "To imagine I were King is pure fiction, merely suggestive, for my first act would be to abdicate." This article inspired my friend, Ralph Bradford, to write a satirical verse in which he portrays to my satisfaction the type of mentality that accounts for the authoritarianism now so enormously on the upswing.

If I were king, I'd abdicate,
Or junk the throne, at any rate . . .
Or maybe I would merely doff
The purple mantle, or leave off
The jeweled crown. . . . For as I muse,
It strikes me I can not refuse
This cup. For who, I ask, am I
The call of duty to deny?
Endowed with gifts that others lack,
It seems to me that I must try
To keep them on the proper track—
To teach them how to earn and spend,
And be most useful in the end.
How can I answer Heaven, pray,
Upon that final Judgment Day,
If I have shirked to do my bit
To make the race of man more fit?
So I shall drink this bitter cup;
Yes, I shall take my burden up,
And work to make men fine and free
And good and true and wise—like me!

Is there a remedy for this egomania? In my judgment
there is one and one only. It was prescribed in the Declara-
tion of Independence:

that all men are . . . endowed by their Creator with certain
unalienable Rights, that among these are Life, Liberty and
the pursuit of Happiness.

We either accept the idea that our rights to quit or start—
our rights to life and liberty—are endowed by the Creator or
we submit to the proposition that they are man-given—in

which case they may be taken back by the giver. There is no other way!

Once any individual grasps this concept, he will quit thinking of himself as almighty and all-wise; he will quit trying to run the lives of others; he will quit his endorsement of all coercive schemes; he will quit acting as other than a normal human being striving to perfect his own life. These are some of the things everyone has a right to quit, a right over which he alone has full control. If we will simply quit meddling with the lives of others, then no longer will "the angels weep."

28

THE ROLE OF
INTERFERENCE

*Determine which actions should be
forcibly halted, and there are the
proper limits of government.*

Current explanations of the limited government concept are
proving inadequate, if not confusing. The lack of progress we
decry should lead not to discouragement but, rather, to new
ways of revealing freedom's superiority to socialism. We obviously have the case, but just as obviously lack the phrasing
that stirs up free market, private ownership, limited government convictions. The proof of our failure to explain may be
seen in our drift or fall into authoritarianism on the one hand,
and into permissiveness and anarchy on the other. It behooves us, therefore, to explore the novel, to look to explanations not yet tried.

Here is one of numerous possibilities that may deserve reflection; and if it seems reasonable, we should refine it as
best we can. *Settle upon those actions which should, and
which should not be, forcibly interfered with and there will*

157

stand in crystal clarity what government should, and should not do.

The essential nature of government is organized force. Back of every law or edict is a constabulary: do as decreed, or else! Government is exclusively an interfering arm of society. Its sole business is forcible interference. This is as it should be. Viewing government's distinctive characteristic in this manner may somewhat simplify our problem: decide what actions of citizens should be subject to forcible interference as distinguished from those actions which should be entirely free from interference. This, at the very least, should make understanding and agreement easier.

To put my thesis in focus I shall, first, suggest a few reasons why so many people forcibly interfere with the lives of others —without even recognizing that they are thus interfering. Secondly, I should like to speculate on how markedly a person's conduct would change for the better were he to regard his obstructive actions for what they really are: interferences!

Today, people by the millions unwittingly interfere with the lives of others for more reasons than we know. Here is a sampling:

- Covetousness undoubtedly heads the list. Envy is an evil that blinds anyone not only to his own blessings but, also, to the rights of others.
- Most people see nothing immoral in feathering their own nests at the expense of their fellow men. They simply have not done their citizenship homework.
- Politicians, "economists," labor officials, clergymen, and even many business leaders, inform us that the communist notion—from each according to ability, to each according to need—is proper and righteous.

- There is a ceaseless bombardment from nearly all media that spending taxpayer's property, for whatever purpose, is the way to prosperity. People, by and large, are not inclined to regard as fallacy that which they wish to believe.
- The lust for power plays an enormous part.
- An unwillingness to think for self when there are those who so graciously offer to do our thinking for us—free of charge!
- The joy of getting on the bandwagon, that is, the desire for popular acclaim.
- The failure to learn from history or to gain understanding from what is going on before our very eyes.
- An alarming lack of faith in a citizenry that is free and self-responsible.
- The silly notion that egalitarianism—bringing the millions to a common level by force—interferences on the grand scale—is our way to the New Jerusalem, the hoped-for Shangri-La.
- Innocent mistakes—community eyesores, pollution, noise nuisances, and the like—which, very often, lead to coercive "cures," interferences more offensive than the original "crimes."

The way to straight thinking on this matter is to reduce the dimension from millions of citizens to a number we can understand: two! In what circumstances would you and I resort to forcible interference, and when would we leave each other alone? This is the only question we need to ask to learn where we really stand and to find out what, in our judgment, is the proper role of government. Big numbers only confuse our thinking; magnitude has nothing whatsoever to do with either morals or principles.

As a starter, would you forcibly interfere were I to threaten your life? I would were you to threaten mine. I would interfere with aggressive violence.

Would you interfere were I to steal from you? I would were you to steal from me. I would interfere with thievery or any form of predation!

Would you interfere were I to use your property rather than mine to express my sympathy for the poor, at home or abroad? I would were you thus to use me. I would interfere with all coercive "charity," whether perpetrated by Robin Hood alone or by his gang.

Would you interfere were I to lie about my service or product? I would were you to do that to me. I would interfere with misrepresentation!

Would you interfere were I to shortchange you? I would were you to defraud me. I would interfere with fraud!

Let us now turn to situations of another nature.

Would you interfere were I to accept a job of waiting on tables for $1.00 an hour? I would not were that your desire. I would not interfere with your choice of a job!

Would you interfere were I to undersell all of my competitors? I would welcome such an achievement by you or anyone else. I would not interfere with free and open competition!

Would you interfere should I prefer to swap my dollars for a foreign product? I would not should that be your choice. I would not interfere with voluntary exchange!

Would you interfere should I grow any crop and in whatever quantity on my own farm? Were that your choice, I would say more power to you. I would not interfere with anyone's peaceful use of his own property!

Would you interfere should I start an airline and make my own rates, be they high or low? I would wish you good fortune if that were your business. I would not interfere with anyone's entry into a business or occupation of his choice at whatever prices he chooses to ask!

Would you interfere were I to work 100 hours a week and for whomever I please? I would encourage you to pursue your own uniqueness, to do as you see fit. I would not interfere with anyone's creative and productive and peaceful efforts!

Enough of these questions. It seems obvious to me that forcible interference is warranted only against the destructive actions of citizens such as violence, predation, misrepresentation, and fraud—injuries imposed on some by others. The limited function of government, therefore, is to codify the taboos —destructive actions, whatever they are—and enforce compliance. Beyond this inhibitory role, there is absolutely nothing that government can do to improve society by bringing its physical force to bear upon individuals.

And it seems just as obvious that all creative activities, without exception, should be left to men acting freely, privately, cooperatively, competitively, voluntarily.

We should always keep in mind that all creative action is spiritual, in the sense that ideas, inventions, discoveries, intuitions, insights are spiritual. Thus it is that everything by which we live and prosper has its inception in the spiritual before ever showing forth in the material. Physical force— forcible interferences—can only deaden, never enliven, the spiritual.

Contrary to the anarchistic position—no government— forcible interference is extremely important and necessary.

That it has a historical record of getting out of bounds is only because of a lack of vigilance and has nothing to do with the propriety of limited government. Out of bounds, it is destructive. In bounds, it permits the flowering of creativity—holds down the bad that the good may flourish.

29

HARMONY UNDERSTOOD

*All discord, harmony not under-
stood.*

—ALEXANDER POPE

All forms of authoritarianism—socialism, state interventionism or welfarism, and the like—are despotic. They are at once
dictatorial, domineering, coercively prescriptive; they are
dogmatic and arrogant. All despotic philosophies may be
simply summarized: "Do as I say, *or else!*" The practices
of this way of life range all the way from one person lording
it over another to those who wield their vast political powers
over millions of citizens. As the eminent German psychiatrist,
Dr. Fritz Kunkel, evaluated this mode of conduct:

> There is not much difference between the medicine-man
> of ten thousand years ago and the political propagandizer
> of our time.[1]

---

[1]See *In Search of Maturity* by Dr. Fritz Kunkel (New York: Charles
Scribner's Sons, 1943), p. 65.

In any event, this despotic way of life—the very antithesis of freedom—rages throughout the world as a forest fire out of control, in the U.S.A. as elsewhere.

True, this political inferno will burn itself out eventually; sooner or later there will be nothing flammable left—no more fuel to sustain the fire. But must we wait out this tiresome historic sequence? Or, does mankind possess the intellectual potential to douse the flames and achieve the noncoercive society in our time? Assuredly, we must try.

Finding the way requires an understanding of, a belief in, and a desire for the free society. Without understanding, belief, and desire, forget it! But granted these intellectual achievements—opening and upgrading the mind to a better idea—all the king's horses and all the king's men are rendered powerless. Sanity wins!

What do I mean by freedom? My most concise, and probably least understood, answer: "no man-concocted restraints against the release of creative human energy." The word "free" has so many different meanings! *The Oxford Dictionary,* for instance, uses over 6,000 words to describe its various connotations. No wonder so few grasp what you or I mean by the free society! The conceptions range from being free of responsibility for self to being free to do anything one pleases regardless of the harm imposed on others, that is, from slavery to anarchy—from *planned* chaos to *unplanned* chaos. We are faced with the old, old problem: not only political tyranny but, also, the tyranny of words!

In any event, the aforementioned ambitious intellectual achievement can never be realized unless we come to some common and acceptable definition of "free." Perhaps it might help to return to the word's original spelling and definition, that is, to medieval English. It was then "freo" and was defined as "to love, to delight, to endear. . . . Not in bondage to another." The freedom philosophy, when rooted in this meaning of "free" makes a great deal of sense to me. At least it deserves analysis and perhaps adoption.

Most of us are content with "Not in bondage to another." I wish to suggest, however, that this, by itself, is a very skimpy definition. If there were no more to freedom than being let alone by others—absence of exterior restraints—we could visualize a society of mummies, not one doing anything against others but, far more significant, not one doing anything helpful to others. If there were no more to the freedom philosophy than this, I would be less enthusiastic than I now am. True, not in bondage is essential to freedom in the sense that not being dead is essential to life. But there is more to life than not being dead and there is more to freedom than not being enslaved.

Continuing the mummy analogy: in the truly free society the mummies come alive. What happens? In one respect, nothing! As mummies, in their new state, they do nothing whatsoever to enslave or injure one another; they remain mummified; not a dictocrat in the population. Then what is changed by reason of their coming alive? Each becomes graced with unimaginable creative aptitudes and potentialities. Interestingly, no two are alike; each one is unique. Joe has skills and talents for this, John for that; the more advanced their skills, the greater the variation; without such variation, men would be mummies. This is to say that were everyone identical to me, all of us would perish. And the same would be true if we were all like you, whoever you are.

What has happened, then, as a result of our freedom to be

different? First, the slightest reflection reveals that all of us have become interdependent. All live on the fruits of each other's labor. Second, we have gained an obligation—dictated by intelligent self-interest—to unmask ourselves, that is, to remove as many inner restraints as possible. Why? That our lights may shine; that our hidden aptitudes and potentialities may emerge. What then is the shape of the free society in its ideal form? It is featured by the absence of both outer and inner restraints. Externally, no one lording it over another! Within, no mummifying self-paralysis hindering the potentially creative self!

Will such an ideal society ever exist? That is, will there ever come a time when individuals will simultaneously (1) refrain from injuring or impairing the rights of others to life, livelihood, liberty and (2) strive for their own intellectual, moral, and spiritual unfoldment? To me, such a possibility is as farfetched as expecting a society of angels. Why, then, spend thought and time defining the ideal, the unattainable? Why not get off "Cloud 9" and return to earth? Why not be "practical"?

Imperfect man's ideal port is, at best, Expectation. Man can sail in the direction of the ideal but this port advances in front of him as he moves toward it. This is not a point of destination but, rather, one of Expectation or Aspiration now and forever. Samuel Johnson phrased it thus:

> It is reasonable to have perfection in the eye that we may always advance toward it, though we know it can never be reached.

I would say that it is not only reasonable to have perfection in the eye but that it is an absolute necessity. In the absence of such a constant star, we are adrift and without compass, all at sixes and sevens—going every which way! The improvement of society—moving in the direction of the ideal—requires, at the very least, a definition of what the ideal is. This is down-to-earth practicality! Why? Because such a definition is the only lodestar we have. Wrote Joel Hawes:

> Aim at the sun, and you may not reach it; but your arrow will fly far higher than if aimed at an object on a level with yourself.

The definition of the ideal society has more to it—much more—than I have so far sketched. Reflect again on the word "free" in its original form, the medieval English "freo." Note that the definition went beyond, "Not in bondage to another" and included "to love, to delight, to endear." What in their time did people mean by this phrasing? Certainly, there was no reference to the free society as we think of it. Society-wise, these people lived under and were aware only of such political establishments as feudalism, serfdom, mercantilism, and the like. The ideal to which we aspire is of recent vintage, ideas and concepts come upon during the past two centuries. To the users of "freo" such concepts as the subjective and marginal utility theory of value, freedom in transactions, private ownership, government limited to keeping the peace were, at best, in embryonic form—not hatched! What, then, did they mean by "to love, to delight, to endear"?

These were family terms—parents to their children and vice versa—that is, to those not enslaved. They loved, were delighted with, and endeared to the few whose relationships were not dictocratic and, thus, not antagonistic. We can infer from this that freo—free—was linked inseparably with and exclusively to *living in harmony*. Here, in my view, was a profound truth in its seedling stage—in embryo! The users of "freo" were unaware of the potential in this seed they were sowing; indeed, most people in today's world are unaware that it has sprouted and grown and flowered; they do not know of the remarkable demonstrations of its efficacy, even though it goes on before their very noses—plus explanations galore. Blind to enlightenments!

This blindness to the fact that freedom and harmony are inseparable twins is easily remedied. Merely do a personal inventory of the persons for whom you have the greatest affection—love, delight, endearment. They will be those, past or present, who enlighten you or, conversely, those who are enlightened by you; in a word, they are those within your circle of light. In the economic realm they will be those who lighten your load and those whose load you lighten.

Wherever and whenever freedom is practiced in the market place, every creative act, whether in goods or services, lightens the load of consumers precisely as it lightens the load of producers. One among countless examples: those who have found out how to raise broilers for prices lower than 50 years ago—and of far higher quality—benefit not only themselves but consumers across the nation. Note how harmonious are these willing exchanges—harmony existing in the absence of antagonisms.

The despotic or interventionist way of life, to the extent it is permitted, generates antagonisms for it rests on the fruitless attempts to do good to some at the expense of others. No injury to any person can ever benefit another. Emerson gave the explanation:

Cause and effect, means and ends, seed and fruit, cannot be severed; for the effect already blooms in the cause, the end pre-exists in the means, the fruit in the seed.

The freedom philosophy is nondespotic and, to the extent of its practice, makes for a harmonious society. How rapidly we move in the direction of this ideal depends on how aptly and quickly we can gain an understanding of, a belief in, and a desire for freedom. By this process, men may deal with one another in harmony rather than discord.

Who can rise to this level of thought? Anyone who is interested and who so wills it. Anyone!

INDEX

Prepared by Vernelia A. Crawford

The letter "n" following a number indicates a footnote.

A

Abundance, 113
Addison, Joseph, 96
Adversity, blessings of, 30-35
Amiel, Henri Frederic, 63, 151
Andrews, Donald Hatch, 2n, 3
Apelles, 24, 25, 29
Aristotle, 58
Authority, 152, 154, 162
Authorship, 32

B

Bacon, Francis, 134
Bailey, Gamaliel, 17
Bastiat, Frederic, 112, 113
Beecher, Henry Ward, 36
Behaviorism, 1-6, 40, 46, 148

Benét, Stephen Vincent, 69
Berger, Peter L., 71n
Bradford, Ralph, 154
Brooks, Van Wyck, 19
Burke, Edmund, 84, 87
Business, private, 89

C

Cause and effect, 169
Chesterton, Gilbert, 69
Chicken Case, 118
Chinese proverb, 45
Civil law, 77
Civilization, measure of, 122
Clark, J. Reuben, Jr., 50
Coleridge, Samuel, 46
Colton, Caleb C., 148
Communication, 45-48

Competition, 98, 100, 113, 117
Compromise, 54-55
Confucius, 104
Consumption and production, 97, 135
Contracts, terms of, 136
Coolidge, Calvin, 122
Creativity, 71, 149
Crowds, 19, 85

D

Decoration Day, 122
Definitions, purpose of, 129
Destiny, fulfillment of, 85
Dillaway, Newton, 8n
Disney, Walt, 93, 96
Drake, Stillman, translator, 24n
Duck hunting, 107

E

Earth, meaning of, 16
Economists, science of, 93
Emerson, Ralph Waldo, 8, 49, 84, 94, 99, 168
Emmons, Nathaniel, 129
Employment, 125, 129-33
Ends and means, 94
Enlightenment, 40
Equality, 76-83
Erasmus, Desiderius, 7, 10
Error, confession of, 49-53
Evil, 115-21
Example, school of mankind, 84, 87
Exchange, voluntary, 82, 97-105

F

Father Joseph, 11n
Fiat money, 135
Folly, railing against, 88-92
Foundation for Economic Education, 43
Franklin, Benjamin, 22, 37, 97, 99, 101, 102
Frederick the Great, 9
Free society, 35, 164-68
Freedom
  benefits and burdens of, 67, 70
  case for, 40
  competition and, 98, 100, 113-17
  definition of, 68
  exchange and, 82, 97-105
  fear of, 68-75
  harmony and, 168
  personal, 97
  privileges of, 147
  return to, 74, 118
  way to, 7-11, 33

G

Gains and losses, 102
Goethe, Johann Wolfgang von, 10, 32, 59, 85, 88-89
Golden Rule, 145-46
Gould, Rowland, 28n
Government
  authority, 152, 154, 162
  coercion, 150
  inflation, 121, 134-41
  limited, 97, 148, 157-62
  nature of, 158

peace-keeping agency, 147
plunder, 95, 140
political controls, 72
programs, 116
protectionism in, 35
social security, 115
socialistic, 34
spending, 134
statesmanship, 89
taxation, 116

H

Habits, 115
Harmony, 162-69
Hare, August, 115
Hawes, Joel, 167
Hayek, F. A., 77
Hazlitt, Henry, 93, 96
Heard, Gerald, 13
Hero-worship, 63
Hickson, W. E., 46
Hinch, Derryn, 109n
Hoover, Herbert, 116
Horace, 30
Horne, George, 78
Human rights, 54
Humility, 7-11, 12
Huxley, Aldous, 11n, 108n
Huxley, Julian, 109n

I

Idolatry, 63
Impatience, 41
Individuals
behaviorism, 1-6, 40, 46, 148
impatience, 41

integrity of, 37, 59
teachable, 14
Industry, 100
Inequality, 76-83
Inflation, 121, 134-41
Integrity, 37, 59
Intellect, appeal to, 36-39
Interference
forcible, 158-62
government, 157-62
impact on, 71
Irreverence, 106

J

Jefferson, Thomas, 118
Jevons, William S., 101-102
Job occupancy, 130
Johnson, Samuel, 166
Judgment, 58

K

Keynes, John Maynard (Lord), 50
Kingship, 148-51
Kunkel, Fritz, 29, 163

L

Labor
conditions of, 124
employment redefined, 125
129-33
glory of, 122-28
job occupancy, 130
profit-sharing, 136

respect for, 127
rights, 152-56
scarcity, 113, 135
unemployment, 125, 129
unions, 125, 154
Law of Attraction, 42
Law of Readiness, 20
Lawbreakers, 119
Leadership, 18
Legal plunder, 95, 140
Legislation, 77, 119
Libyan decree, 153-54
Life insurance, 28
Life styles, 17-23
Longfellow, Henry Wadsworth, 17
Lorenz, Konrad Z., 109n

M

Mackay, Charles, 19n
Manufacturing, 97
Masses, 19, 85
Means and ends, 169
Meekness, 12-16
Memorial Day, 122
Menger, Carl, 101-102
Minding one's business, 25
Mises, Ludwig von, 83n, 104
Mistakes, 49-53
Money theories, 50, 135
Montaigne, Michel, 101
Morality, 104
Mummy analogy, 165
Mystery in creation, 8
Mythology, 112

N

National Industrial Recovery Act, 117, 120
Nature
characteristics of, 59
equality and, 76, 78
truth and, 85

O

Obstacles, mastery of, 32
Oil companies, foreign, 152
Oleomargarine, 117
Opinions, reflections on, 45-48
Osler, William, 126
Ownership, 142-47

P

Perfection, 166
Peter and Paul, 84, 86
Plato, 85
Plunder, 95, 140
Plutarch, 30, 49
Political controls, 72
Politicians, errors of, 51
Pope, Alexander, 162
Potentialities, 16
Production, 97, 135
Profit-sharing, 136
Prohibition, 116, 118
Prosperity, 30
Protectionism, 35
Purchasing power, 135

R

Radiation, art of, 47
Ratner, Joseph, 84n
Readiness, law of, 20-23
Reason vs. unreason, 88
Reflection, art of, 45
Restraint, impact on, 71
Reverence, importance of, 104-11
Richelieu, Cardinal, 11n
Right and wrong, 1-6, 57, 104
Right to quit, 152-56
Roosevelt, Franklin, 115, 117, 120
Rostand, Edmond, 59
Runes, Dagobert D., editor, 64n
Russia, job occupancy in, 130

S

Sanford, Lloyd, 108
Santayana, George, 142
Say's Law, 135
Scarcity, 104, 113, 135
Schiller, Johann C. F., 18
Schmidt, Emerson, 115n
Schweitzer, Albert, 106n, 108, 110
Socrates, 1, 65, 80
Self-analysis, 1
Selfhood, 143
Self-improvement, 40, 46
Self-interest, 138-40
Self-responsibility, 73
Self-revelation, 84-87
Selye, Hans, 127
Service, Robert, 31

Shakespeare, William, 23, 40, 59, 106, 108, 152
Shoemaker, 24-29
Sisyphus, 112-14
Sixteenth Amendment, 116
Slavery, 131-32, 142-45
Social security, 115
Socialism, 34
Society, good, structuring, 24-29
Sound, speed of, 14
Specialization, 81, 124
Spending, government, 134
Spinoza, Benedictus, 84-87
Statesmanship, 89
Stealing, 56, 94, 105, 145-46
Sumner, Charles, 54
Supply and demand, 138
Surrender, penalty of, 54-62

T

Talents, 20, 30
Tariffs, 100
Taxation, progressive, 116
Ten Commandments, 57
Theft, 56, 94, 105, 145-46
Thoreau, Henry David, 4, 12
Time-lapse thinking, 93-96
Tocqueville, Alexis de, 73
Tottle, John, 99n
Trade, reflections on, 82, 97-105
Truth
  discovery of, 40-44
  merit in, 64
  Nature and, 85
  search for, 38, 41, 91
Tryanny, political, 74

U

Unemployment, 125, 129
Unions, labor, 125, 154
Unreason, 88

V

Vanvenargues, Marguis de, 76
Vested interest, 121, 139
Viewpoints, 45-48
Violence, 153

Voice, within and without, 47
Volstead Act, 116, 118

W

Walras, Léon, 101-102
Weakness, appeal to, 36
Webster, Daniel, 99
Williams, Roger J., 78n
Wilson, Woodrow, 116
Wisdom, lesson of, 49
Worship, 63-67